Amazing but True
Golf Facts

By Allan Zullo

Astonishing but True Golf Facts

By Chris Rodell

*Hole in One! The Complete Book of Fact,
Legend, and Lore of Golf's Luckiest Shot*

Amazing but True
Golf Facts

Allan Zullo and Chris Rodell

**Andrews McMeel
Publishing**

Kansas City

Book design by Pete Lippincott

04 05 06 07 BID 10 9 8 7 6 5 4 3 2

Library of Congress Cataloging-in-Publication Data
Zullo, Allan.
    Amazing but true golf facts / Allan Zullo and Chris Rodell.
       p.cm.
    ISBN 0-7407-3860-7
    1. Golf—Miscellanea. 2. Golf—Humor. I. Rodell, Chris. II. Title.
GV967.Z84 2003
796.352—dc21
                                                          2003050303

Contents

Tee Time   1

The Good, the Bad, and the Ugly   3

Mishaps and Misdemeanors   23

Incidents of Ignobility   40

Ace in the Hole   56

Hot Shots   73

Inside the Ropes   93

Flak and Fuss   124

Head Games   140

Par for the Course   159

Right on the Money   188

Duffers and Hackers   204

Fandemonium   221

Bag of Sticks   234

Toter Talk   247

Holing Out   257

Tee Time

AFTER THE BOOK *Astonishing but True Golf Facts* was published in 2001, it became quite obvious that there was a need for another book about more incredible incidents, hilarious happenings, fantastic feats, and remarkable records in golf. Let's face it, the game of golf has given us so much to talk—and write—about.

This book chronicles a sampling of the people, places, and events in golf that we hope will intrigue and fascinate you. The book features such unusual facts as:

- The pro who, during an exhibition, landed more than 1,500 drives within a 30-yard circle, missing the target just eight times

Amazing but True Golf Facts

- The Tour player who won a tournament after his wayward drive struck his fiancée and bounced back onto the fairway
- The penny that cost a Tour player $100,000 in lost earnings
- The wife of a Tour player who sent a man dressed in a gorilla suit to cheer up her slumping husband
- The 101-year-old golfer who shot a hole in one
- The power golfer who can slam a golf ball through a phone book and a ¾-inch piece of plywood

From munis to championship courses, golf will continue to amaze, confound, and delight us—just as this new collection of fascinating facts hopes to do.

The Good, the Bad, and the Ugly

TIGER WOODS HAD A REMARKABLE three-shot run during a practice round at Spain's Valderrama Golf Club in 2000.

It began when he holed a 110-yard eagle from the fairway on the third hole. Feeling that he was in a groove, he asked his caddie to drop a ball into a greenside bunker to see if he (Tiger) could hole that one too. He did. So he asked his caddie to throw the ball back into the bunker again. Incredibly, he holed it again!

During the 1939 U.S. Open, Byron Nelson hit the pin six times from the tee or the fairway.

But not one of those shots dropped into the cup for an ace or an eagle. The shots were struck with six different clubs—wedge, nine-iron, six-iron, four-iron, one-iron and driver. The bad luck led to a tie and an 18-hole Monday playoff, which Nelson won with a 70 that included a pin-clicking eagle on the par-4 fourth hole. Nelson said that had he lost, it would have been one of the most frustrating losses of his career.

John Francis is the father of the Scottsdale, Arizona, golf prodigy Philip Francis, winner of four Junior World Championships and one of the most promising youths in golf history.

Still, the father may have achieved something the son never will—a double eagle on a 625-yard hole that's just 22 yards shy of the world record. It happened in 1989 at Skyland Country Club in Crested Butte, Colorado, when his second shot went in on the fly.

"I hit that second shot and, man, it really had some steam on it," Francis recalled. "It was so far away I couldn't see it, but I saw the maintenance guys in the back of the green going crazy. I got up there and they told me it hit on the fly. It broke the back of the cup and stayed in."

The event is so rare most mathematicians bust their calculators simply trying to compute the astronomical odds of two playing partners each acing the same hole.

But what's even more rare is when each playing partner nails an eagle on the same par-4. That's what Gary Gross and Boyd Cox of Fayetteville, Arkansas, achieved at the 371-yard par-4 second hole at Fayetteville Country Club on November 11, 2002. Cox eagled the hole with a six-iron from 150 yards out. Moments later, Gross knocked his second shot into the cup with a seven-iron from 140 yards out.

Amazing but True Golf Facts

ESPN SportsCenter host Stuart Scott was with Tiger Woods the day he filmed his famous bounce-the-ball-on-the-end-of-the-club commercial for Nike.

Scott recalled that while they were waiting for the crew to set up, Woods said, "Bet I can chip a ball off that railing over there and make it bounce into that trash can." Woods did just that.

But when it came time to shoot the commercial, Tiger was having trouble maintaining the bouncing ball on his club. Finally, a cameraman taunted him, "Aren't you supposed to be the best golfer in the world?"

Scott recalled, "Now Tiger gets that look in his eye: 'Give me the ball.' *Bop, bop, bop* for exactly thirty seconds and then–*wham!*–he hits it on a line about a hundred fifty yards."

Golf magazine called it the best recovery shot of 2001. It happened at the Invensys Classic in Las Vegas when Bob Estes hit a ball that lodged in a bush on the 6th hole of the final round. Instead of declaring his ball unplayable, Estes swung at it with a driver and rapped it cleanly out to where he had a clean shot at the green. He ended up holing a 45-foot par putt and went on to shoot a 63 and win the event.

Tiger Woods says it was the best shot he'd ever hit. Few who remember it will disagree.

It happened during the rain-delayed second round of the 2002 PGA Championship at Hazeltine National in Chaska, Minnesota. After pulling his drive into the soggy par-4 fairway bunker on the 18th hole, Woods was faced with 202 yards to the pin, an uphill shot with the ball severely below his feet. To make matters more difficult, he had to clear a stand of trees protecting the green.

Rather than pitch safely to the front of the green, Woods, who'd already won two of the three major championships for the year, pulled out a three-iron and took a swing that would have made Paul Bunyan proud. The ball cleared the lip, the trees and another greenside bunker, and then landed softly on the green, amazingly, just 12 feet away. Woods sank the birdie putt on what seemed to be pure adrenaline.

Woods wound up finishing second, one stroke behind the winner, Rich Beem.

Yes, Phil Mickelson actually practices his famous "backward flop" shot that was filmed for a 2001 KPMG (now called Bearing Point) commercial.

In the ad, Mickelson has his back to the green, hits the ball backward over the head of company CEO Rand Blazer . . . and into the cup. In case you're wondering, it was done on the third take.

Flabbergasted probably isn't a strong enough word to describe the reaction John Daly had when Costantino Rocca made a long snaky putt through the Valley of Sin at the 18th at St. Andrews to send the 1995 British Open into a playoff.

Moments earlier, Daly was ready to celebrate after watching Rocca flub a chip that left him a 65-foot putt to tie. Incredibly, Rocca made the putt and sent the championship into a five-hole playoff that Daly won after Rocca took a 7 on the fourth playoff hole.

To this day, when asked what the greatest shot he's ever seen in golf was, Daly says it was Rocca's putt.

The shot and the run that preceded it were so remarkable that to this day many fans still confuse Steve Lowery with the actual winner of the 2002 International at Castle Pines Country Club. Under the Stableford scoring system, Lowery earned big points by birdieing from the bank of a greenside pond on number 14. Then he holed a 127-yard wedge for eagle on number 15. Still, the showstopper came at 17, when Lowery holed a six-iron from 190 yards to double-eagle the par-5 17th hole.

What no one remembers is that Lowery couldn't sink a 12-foot birdie putt on 18 and lost the shooting match to Rich Beem, who used the win as a launching pad to the PGA Championship victory at Hazeltine National.

Ask any Tour player about the hardest shot they've ever seen hit and they'll say, "The one Tiger hit at . . ." and mention a gallery of amazing shots from Pebble, Firestone, Muirfield, and a dozen other epic locales. What about when you ask Woods? He'll tell you about the time in the late 1980s when he saw someone at a Nike tournament hit a five-iron that was so hard it knocked the ball out of round. The striker? Big John Daly.

Moe Norman was considered the best ball striker ever by many golf purists, including Lee Trevino, Tom Watson, and Sam Snead. He was also, without a doubt, one of golf's greatest eccentrics.

Norman often slept overnight in bunkers on the course, drank a case of Coke a day, and eventually quit the PGA Tour because his squirrel-like chattering drove other players nuts.

Still, club pros teach his so-called "natural golf swing" to his admirers who want to learn his secret. For Norman, it was a secret he discovered at the age of 19 and sharpened over a lifetime. "At nineteen, I had my move down. It felt so good. I thought, 'Keep this and make it stronger.'"

Norman hit the same swing time after time. He supposedly used the same tee for more than 10 years. He once held an exhibition where he landed more than 1,500 drives within a 30-yard circle, missing the target just eight times.

The Good, the Bad, and the Ugly

The veteran golf writer T. R. Reinman recalls meeting Phil
Mickelson when the kid was just 14. Reinman bet Mickelson
a Coke that he (Reinman) could hit a driving-range fence
250 yards out, which he did. Then Mickelson bet him two
Cokes that he (Mickelson) could do it with any club in
Reinman's bag, even though the writer is right-handed and
Mickelson is a lefty. Mickelson pulled out Reinman's driver,
turned it so the toe of the club faced down, and smacked the
ball 250 yards left-handed. The lesson? Don't bet with
Mickelson when he's thirsty.

Scott Hoch has put together one of the finest careers in golf,
winning more than $16 million between 1980 and 2002, but
even he knows he'll be forever marked as the guy who missed
a two-and-a-half-foot putt to lose the 1989 Masters.

When asked how he should be defined, he said, "Good player. Missed that putt at the Masters. Should've won a big one, never did. That Masters will always be the one."

Nick Price was a boy in the hood during the 2002 Masters when his tee shot at number 15 took a crazy bounce off a man's shoulder and landed in the hood of a female spectator.

The location entitled Price to a free drop from where the ball came to rest—and it was still in her hood as Price and the rules official hashed out the decision.

Looking to take advantage of the situation, Price motioned the woman to the center of the fairway and joked, "Would you stand over here, please?"

The Good, the Bad, and the Ugly

Tom Watson says the feeling he gets from watching his tee shot go into Rae's Creek on the 12th hole at Augusta National is like watching a horror movie—only this horror is happening to you.

"Have you seen that movie *Alien*, where the creature comes out of your chest?" Watson asks. "Well, that's what it feels like on 12 when that happens."

Watson hit two balls in the water and took a quadruple-bogey 7 there in 2002.

For Tim Herron, the punishment for a bad shot was more than losing any hope of winning the 2003 Bob Hope Classic. It also involved hard labor and mortification.

While holding a four-shot lead down the stretch of the final round, Herron mis-hit a shot from a bunker that flew past the 16th green and landed in some dastardly rock outcroppings that line the Palmer Course at PGA West. Herron was allowed to drop after taking an unplayable lie stroke, but his troubles were just beginning. He cleared out a large, heavy patch of rocks and twigs that were deemed loose impediments. Still, he couldn't bulldoze enough away to give himself a workable shot. His still-rocky lie caused him to skull his shot into the canal fronting the green on his way to a quadruple-bogey 8 and an eventual tie for third.

That bunker shot cost him about $550,000—the difference between the winner's prize of $810,000 and his earnings of $261,000 for finishing in a third-place tie.

Neville Rowlandson, an amateur golfer, hit a shot that can top any hole in one. He got what *Golf World* magazine called a "course-in-one."

In 2002, Rowlandson, 56, skulled his tee shot on the first hole at the Felixstowe Ferry Golf Club in Suffolk, England. The ball struck a tee marker in front of the tee, ricocheted to the right, bounded 25 yards, struck the pin on number 18—and dropped into the cup!

As Rowlandson stood there dumbstruck and embarrassed by what had just happened, his caddie said to him, "Congratulations, you've just set a new course record."

When the astronaut Alan Shepard decided to make the moon his golf course during his 1971 *Apollo 14* lunar walk, his little stunt set the taxpayers back about $12,000. That's how much it cost to take about two pounds of cargo into space.

Shepard smuggled a six-iron clubhead and two golf balls inside an old sweat sock. A 12 handicapper on Earth, the astronaut wanted to be the first man on the moon to hit a golf ball. So when all the work on the moon was completed, he attached the clubhead to a shaftlike device that had been used by the crew to collect lunar dust samples.

It was a golfer's worst nightmare because the moon was one big sand trap. Unfortunately, with the whole world watching, Shepard chili-dipped golf's first space shot . . . and shanked his second shot.

The sock and clubhead, along with the tool he screwed the clubhead onto, are today in the United States Golf Association Museum in Far Hills, New Jersey.

When Hubert Green missed a three-foot putt on the last hole of the 1978 Masters to miss out on a playoff with Gary Player, he returned to the exact spot later that night after the festivities had concluded. He tried five putts from the same spot and missed them all. Then he picked up his ball and left.

In golf, one shot can haunt your whole life, as Doug Sanders is still so painfully aware.

He missed a three-foot putt on the final green at St. Andrews that would have made him the 1970 British Open champion. Because of the miss, he forced an 18-hole playoff with Jack Nicklaus the next day. He lost the playoff by a stroke, 72–73.

Admits Sanders, "When I tell people I can go 10 minutes without thinking about it, I'm exaggerating . . . but only a little."

Sanders figures his life would have been vastly different had the putt dropped. In that regard, he's probably right on target.

Twice Bernhard Langer has been out on a limb in pursuit of errant shots.

During a tournament in England in 1982, his second shot on the 4th hole disappeared into a big oak tree near the green. Spectators did not see it come down. A close look revealed the ball was lodged in a little indentation on a huge branch about 15 feet above the ground.

Langer debated whether he should take the penalty shot or climb up into the tree and hit it. He decided to go for it. Recalled Langer: "I hit the ball from up in the tree onto the green and the crowd went absolutely crazy. The TV cameras had everything on tape and hours later the picture of me hitting the ball out of the tree went around the world. Two days later I flew to Akron, Ohio, to play in the World Series of Golf tournament, which was my first ever event in the United States. I was coleader after three rounds and I heard the people in the crowd saying, 'There's the guy who was up in the tree.'"

The Good, the Bad, and the Ugly

Nearly 20 years later, at the 2001 Williams World Challenge in California, an unofficial tournament hosted by Tiger Woods, Langer sent a wayward shot into a large oak tree. This time, he chose not to climb up and hit the ball from the tree. Instead, he shook the ball loose. Langer took a penalty stroke and managed to save par.

Kirk Nelson, a 43-year-old Hawaiian club pro, got a taste of life in the spotlight when, during the 2003 Sony Open, he hit a 256-yard three-wood second shot to the 18th green during the first round. The shot was so well struck, producers decided to show it for Nelson and all to see on the giant Jumbotron screen behind the green. For Nelson, however, the glory was short-lived. "I got so excited watching the replay, I three-putted for par," Nelson recalled.

In 1934 at St. Margaret's-at-Cliffe Golf Club, Kent, England, W. J. Robinson, the club professional, had a beef after hitting a wayward drive on the 18th hole. His ball struck a cow in the back of the head. When Robinson and his playing partners reached the heifer, she was dead.

Mishaps and Misdemeanors

PROS, NO MATTER HOW PAMPERED, aren't immune to getting plunked by errant balls. Frank Nobilo was playing a round at Lake Nona Golf and Country Club near Orlando in 1998 when a ball whacked him above the left eye.

Luckily for Nobilo, there was a doctor in the vicinity—the guy who whacked the ball. The gash required 30 stitches. The accident left Nobilo wearing an eyepatch for a short time, a fitting look for a man who is a descendant of a marauding Italian pirate.

The pro golfer Jonathan Byrd accidentally hit his fiancée with an errant tee shot during the final round at the 2002 Buick Challenge—but it turned out to be a good thing. Very good.

As his ball was heading out of bounds, it whizzed into the gallery, where it struck Amanda Talley on the left shoulder and bounced on the cart path and onto a favorable lie in the rough on the fifth hole. When he found out she was okay, he said, "Thanks!"

Byrd went on to win the tournament by one stroke, becoming the seventeenth first-time winner on Tour in 2002.

A month after the incident, the blushing bride and the bruising groom were married.

South Africa's Retief Goosen described himself as "a bit shocked" at winning the 2001 U.S. Open playoff, and if ever there is a guy who knows the difference between being "a bit shocked" and "a bunch shocked," it is Goosen.

The South African was 17 when he was struck by lightning while golfing, in 1986. "It's a sight I'll never forget," recalled his cousin, Henri Potgieter, who was playing with him at the time. "Retief's clothes had burned off his body—even his underpants. The smell of burning hair was overpowering. I was sure he was dead."

Goosen overcame many health problems resulting from the lightning strike to become an international star.

Lightning struck, literally and figuratively, at the 1991 PGA Championship when an unknown golfer named John Daly drove through the night from Memphis to Crooked Stick Golf Club in Carmel, Indiana, to claim the last position in the tournament.

He played and won without ever seeing the course before and without the benefit of a practice round. Sadly, the event was marred by an actual lightning strike that claimed the life of a gallery patron. Daly donated $30,000 of his winnings, his first significant check as a professional, to the family of the lightning-strike victim.

Most everyone dreams of owning a home fronting a golf course, but for some that dream can become a nerve-wracking nightmare. Just ask Jeff and Ellie Ward of Stow, Ohio.

Their home sits adjacent to the number 3 teebox at the Roses Run Country Club, and is directly in the line of fire for golfers looking to shorten the dogleg of the 385-yard par-4 fourth hole. Since the couple moved into the house in 1995, more than 100 balls have bombarded it each year.

"We knew the house would get hit by a few golf balls when we moved in," Ellie said. "Granted, we didn't know how many, but we've learned to live with it."

Still, it gets a little galling when golfers use it for target practice. "I heard one guy standing on the tee telling a guy the strategy for the 4th hole," Jeff said. "The one golfer pointed toward our house and said, 'See that house? Now, just hit it over the porch and you'll have a shot at the green.' It was all I could do to bite my tongue."

Many pros keep an unlikely and ill-advised medicinal aid in their bags for emergencies like the one John Daly had during the 2001 British Open. An old wound on his hand reopened and forced him to have surgery.

The doctors advised him not to swing a club until the wound had healed. It was advice Daly ignored. So when the blood started gushing again while he was playing, he stopped it by closing the cut with Superglue. "I don't care if that's unwise medically," he said. "I'm not going to watch it bleed."

Golfers are notorious for their gallows humor. It goes with the territory.

Take, for example, the true story of the golfer who, while playing a round at the Cedars of Bergstrom course near Austin, Texas, suffered a heart attack. The emergency medical service was called. While in the throes of cardiac arrest, the golfer uttered what might very well have been his last words. "Watch my Pings," he told his playing partners.

As paramedics were loading him into an ambulance, his golfer friends showed their concern as only golfers can. "You're not getting off that easy," one said. "You still owe five dollars for the skins game."

Mishaps and Misdemeanors

A violent downpour nearly killed the course architect Jay Morrish—and yet probably saved his life.

Morrish was outside working on a new course design near Tucson, Arizona, when ominous clouds suddenly opened up and drenched the area with a downpour that caused flash floods. Morrish ran through the driving rain to his hotel room. It was several more minutes before he realized just how lucky he was to have escaped alive—and not only from the storm.

"I stuck my hand into my boot to oil it and pricked my finger," he recalled. "A rattlesnake had bitten through my boot and even reached clear to my sock. But because I was running, the fangs snapped right off. Somewhere out there, some snake is gumming rabbits."

In 1997 the actor Michael Douglas was sued for $155 million by a caddie, James Parker, who claimed Douglas smacked him in the groin with an errant golf ball—an alleged "screaming liner"—during a tournament at the Elmwood Country Club in White Plains, New York. According to the lawsuit, "[T]he plaintiff noticed that defendant Douglas was becoming restless. It was his turn to tee off. Parker proceeded down the course as he had previously done on each previous hole played. However, before he reached a safe distance on the green, defendant Douglas hit his golf ball. . . . Plaintiff Parker heard the sound of a golf ball, turned around and as he tried to lower himself to the ground was struck in his penis and testicles by the golf ball and was unable to move."

Parker said Douglas stuffed money in the caddie's pocket to cover his pain and suffering. The caddie claimed that because of the wayward shot, he suffered an inflamed penis and had a ruptured testicle that needed to be removed surgically. The injuries, he said, kept him from working.

Douglas settled for $2 million.

Mishaps and Misdemeanors

A golfer at Donald Trump's Palm Beach golf retreat got the most expensive birdie on record in 2001.

He was ordered to pay $2,500 to an animal rescue league and $800 in court costs after clubbing an exotic black swan to death with his driver. The golfer maintained he killed the swan to defend other golfers.

Two thieves sneaked into the locker room at Sherwood Country Club, where Tiger Woods was hosting the 2002 Target World Challenge. They each managed to steal a club out of Tiger's locker.

Then they tried to blend in by shooting pool in the clubhouse with Rich Beem, who, in between billiard shots, found himself admiring the two clubs. He thought they were pro-am prizes and didn't see the "TW" stamped on the bottom. But someone else did and the thieves were busted.

Scott Laycock, a Tour rookie in 2003, learned a costly lesson about the Tour's no-cart policy at the 2003 Sony Open in Hawaii.

He was playing a brisk round when nature called. The only problem was that the nearest comfort station was in the greenskeeper's compound. Worried about slowing up play and incurring a penalty, Laycock accepted a ride in a cart and heeded nature's call. Upon returning to play, Tour official Mike Shea told him carts were allowed only in cases of emergency, such as diarrhea. Laycock confessed it wasn't that serious. That's when Shea assessed him a two-stroke penalty for using the cart. "That did give me the diarrhea," Laycock said.

Greg Norman's famous collapse at the 1996 Masters had something in common with the assassination of Abraham Lincoln in 1865 and the sinking of the *Titanic* in 1912. All three events happened on April 14.

What happened to Norman that day wasn't all that bad. He still got to play a round at Augusta and he became a role model for graciousness in defeat by showing the world how a true sportsman dealt with adversity. Not a bad day after all.

An honest coach with an eagle eye stripped his team of a championship—while the team was taking pictures with the trophy.

In 2002, a Westborough (Massachusetts) High School coach, Greg Rota, was looking over the scorecards at the state Division II championships after his team had been awarded the trophy when he noticed that one player had mistakenly written a 7 where a 9 should have been on the final hole in the team's match against rival Woborn High School.

Although none of the scoring officials seemed to have noticed the error, Rota immediately told his team to stop posing for pictures and had the correct score posted. The error turned a one-stroke victory into a one-stroke defeat.

Later that week, it was the Woburn team who posed for the championship pictures. But the Westborough golfers came out of this situation with something pretty valuable too—a lesson in honesty.

Golfer David Hartshorne's failure to qualify at the 2002 New Zealand Open left him in a foul mood. It wasn't his game; it was a ruling that he thought stank.

Hartshorne, a professional from Lower Hutt in New Zealand's North Island, was eliminated from prequalifying competition when he missed a 35-foot putt on the first hole of a three-way playoff. His request for relief from duck droppings in the line of his putt was refused by Phil Aickin, the New Zealand Open tournament director and referee.

Hartshorne argued that the duck droppings were a loose impediment, which he could lift or brush aside. Not so, according to Aickin, who said, "Fresh dung will sit there a couple of centimeters high, but once somebody stands on it, it flattens and gets baked to the green."

Before the third round of the 2001 Kemper Insurance Open, Australian Greg Chalmers noticed that a caddie from his group had peered into Chalmers's bag. The Aussie was irked but didn't say anything because the caddie did nothing illegal, although it wasn't very fair.

Later in the round, Chalmers hit a bad tee shot and another caddie tried to look at his club, causing Chalmers to snap, "I hit a six-iron. Just get away from me."

Technically, Chalmers had violated a rule because his statement "I hit a six-iron" was giving someone advice. He should have given himself a two-stroke penalty.

But Chalmers did not realize his mistake until later that night. Being an honest man, he went to the rules committee before the final round and told his story. Because he forgot to penalize himself for giving advice, it meant he had signed an incorrect scorecard for that round. So he had to disqualify himself. Chalmers was tied for twelfth place at the time. Had he finished the final round in the same place, he would've pocketed $95,000.

The caddie, by the way, did not violate a rule. He just received advice. If he had asked for advice, his golfer would have been subject to a penalty.

When they say something is a hazard in South Africa, they really mean it's a hazard. Same goes for the words "Keep out."

Graeme Francis didn't know that disobeying a local rule could have cost him more than a stroke—it could have cost him his life. During the Dimension Data Pro-Am in South Africa in 2001, Francis was disqualified after playing a ball from an active crocodile pit. There were no crocodiles present, but a local rule—not to mention common sense—prohibits golfers from playing through the pit.

A penny cost Paul Gow over $100,000.

Gow angrily tossed down the coin, which he had been using as a marker, after missing a short putt on the 11th hole at the 2001 B.C. Open.

The coin inadvertently struck his ball and moved it, costing Gow a one-stroke penalty. That one extra stroke meant the difference between Gow's winning the tournament outright and tying Jeff Sluman, resulting in a playoff that Sluman won.

The errant toss wound up costing Gow a whopping $144,000—the difference in prize money between finishing first and second.

"I missed a putt for par," Gow explained. "I was a few feet away and threw my penny down and it moved the ball an inch—it was a real good shot."

Mishaps and Misdemeanors

Colin Montgomerie was declared out of bounds when, during an off week in which he'd skipped the 2001 BellSouth Classic, he showed up anyway and started working out on the driving range for a few hours of practice.

A Tour official finally told him that rules prohibit players who are not participating in a tournament from practicing at the site. He was asked to leave, and did.

Incidents of Ignobility

TIGER WOODS OWES A DEBT of gratitude to a waitress for helping him win the 2000 Canadian Open.

He almost was disqualified for missing the start of the round because he and his caddie thought tee time was 8:57 A.M., instead of 7:57 A.M.

Woods was in a restaurant waiting for an omelet, unaware that his playing partners were on the practice range getting ready. Luckily the waitress was thinking for Woods, he explained afterward. "The lady came up to me and says, 'Well, you have fifteen minutes until your tee time.'"

He raced out to the course and made it to the first tee with only a minute to spare.

Incidents of Ignobility

Former PGA Tour player Mike Reasor holds a record for ignominy. He shot the highest total ever for the final two rounds of a PGA tournament.

Just hours after making the cut at the 1974 Tallahassee Open, Reasor went horseback riding. But he was thrown from his horse and suffered several injuries. He separated his shoulder, damaged knee ligaments, and tore rib cartilage. After being treated at the hospital, he insisted on finishing the tournament to maintain eligibility for the following week's event and also to pick up a guaranteed paycheck. Swinging just a five-iron one-handed, Reasor shot a woeful 123 and 114. But at least he finished the tourney.

The sky-high rounds weren't his only claim to golfing ignominy. It was Reasor who caddied for Arnold Palmer during the 1966 U.S. Open in which Palmer blew a final-round seven-stroke lead and eventually lost to Billy Casper in an 18-hole playoff at the Olympic Club in San Francisco.

South African pro Hennie Otto had a three-week stretch in 2001 that would make any golfer in his shoes think about taking up tennis instead.

He shot a horrible second-round 80 at the South African Masters that so infuriated him, he threw his clubs into a river. Then the next week, he erupted in rage after blowing a third-round lead at the South African Open with an awful 77 that left him in fifth place. He followed that poor outing by being disqualified from the South African PGA for signing an incorrect scorecard.

On a scorecard that could please only a bored mathematician with a broken calculator, David Terpoilli of West Norristown, Pennsylvania, wrote a "1" at the 128-yard 16th hole on his way to shooting, gulp, 123-over 193 at Whitemarsh Country Club in October 1994.

Incidents of Ignobility

The scorecard's back nine read: 9-21-9-16-11-13-1-11-9–100. The beauty of it is that no one who ever wrote "21" for one hole could ever be accused of lying about his ace five holes later.

◉

Tiger Woods was asked about putting woes that kept him from winning every single tournament in which he was entered as was expected. Announcers and golf writers emptied their vocabularies to explain how he was leaving putts achingly short or, worse, rimming them without hearing the click in the cup. Woods, an economist, used just one word. He said he was suffering from "liprosy."

◉

Gary McCord earned a berth on the CBS announcing crew after an admittedly undistinguished career on the PGA Tour.

McCord played on the Tour 17 years without a single Tour victory.

When McCord met golf legend Ben Hogan and told him he was a professional Tour player, Hogan was puzzled that he didn't know McCord's name. When he found out McCord's less-than-illustrious record, Hogan replied, "Seventeen years and no wins? What the hell are you even out there for? You need to get a job."

McCord has a California vanity license plate that reads, "NO WINS."

Fans at the 2002 WGC-NEC Invitational in Sammamish, Washington, were surprised to see Rich Beem flubbing shots out of a bunker just days after he'd held off Tiger Woods to win the PGA Championship, his first major.

During the first round, some of Beem's shots were so ugly one fan asked out loud what many of the others were thinking.

Seeing Beem blow a sand shot, the heckler called out sarcastically, "That's the guy who just won the PGA last week?"

Beem responded honestly and somewhat sheepishly, "I didn't hit many bunkers last week." After shooting a woeful 74, Beem showed his championship form by firing three straight 67s to finish sixth.

At the beginning of the 2002 PGA Tour season, Jesper Parnevik told his wife, Mia, that he wasn't coming home until he won on Tour. She waited six weeks for him to finish atop the leader board, but he couldn't swing it.

To keep his spirits up and to let him know she was still behind him, Mia hired a man in a gorilla suit to serenade Parnevik on the practice range at the Riviera Country Club at the Nissan Open. The ape sang "Close to You," by the

Carpenters, with an accompaniment of fellow Tour pros and caddies.

Unfortunately, though, the rest of the players made a monkey out of Parnevik, and he went winless for the seventh consecutive week. In fact, Parnevik didn't win once that year. He chose not to send Mia a guy in a gorilla suit to sing the Beatles tune "I'm a Loser."

The nail-biter finish to regulation play at the 2001 U.S. Open at Southern Hills Country Club in Tulsa proved a headline writer's dream. In contention were colorfully named players Stewart Cink and the eventual winner, Retief Goosen, and both blew putts on the final hole. Their performance inspired lots of fun headlines. Some of the offerings included "Chokelahoma!" and "Duck! Duck! Goosen" and, finally, "Stewart Sinks When He Can't!"

After his retirement, Ty Cobb tried desperately to attain the same level of success in golf that he had reached in baseball. It was a frustration that would haunt him to his grave.

His most humiliating moment came during the 1939 Olympic Club championship when he lost to a 12-year-old prodigy and future announcer, Bob Rosburg. "I beat him badly," Rosburg recalled. "He cleaned out his locker and never returned to Olympic."

They don't intend it to happen that way, and they really love their fans, but sometimes pros will let loose with a drive knowing it might carom off a spectator's noggin and back onto the fairway.

During the 2001 Bay Hill Classic, Tiger Woods said he wasn't too worried when he drove a ball out of bounds. "With that many people over there," he said, "it was more than likely going to smoke somebody." It did, which kept the ball safely in bounds. Woods went on to win the tournament.

The PGA encourages its Tour players to be models of comportment: no swearing, no trash talking, no titanic tantrums. That's why it has nice guys like Brad Faxon on the Tour Policy Board, someone other players can look to as an even-tempered example of how to play the game. But golf can get the better of anyone. Even someone like Faxon, who's supposed to set a good example.

Incidents of Ignobility

He remembers one awful round with Hubert Green at the BellSouth Classic when nothing would go right. "I was slowly losing my way," Faxon told *Golf Digest*. "Nothing was going my way. I bogeyed the 12th hole—missed the green and maybe even made a double—and I just took my golf bag and chucked it down the hill. I was so upset."

That's when Green came up and added confusion to Faxon's feelings of anger. Green said, "I'm proud of you." When Faxon asked why, Green said, "I didn't think you had it in you. I thought you were too nice. That's a positive."

Another time, Faxon suffered a back-nine meltdown that dropped him from third place to twentieth at the Byron Nelson Classic. He waited until he was back at his room at the pricey Four Seasons near Irving, Texas, before losing his temper. Faxon tossed a chair that hit a painting and smashed the glass frame into a million pieces.

When he calmed down, he sheepishly called the hotel's general manager and asked, "Are you a golfer?" The G.M. said he was. Faxon then confessed, telling his troubles on the course and explaining how his frustration led to the damage of a painting worth a thousand dollars.

Recalled Faxon, "I told him, 'I'm happy to pay for it.' And he said, 'No, I totally understand.' That was the last time I ever lost it."

Paul Azinger spent the back nine of the 1996 British Open at Royal Lytham and St. Anne's putting with a sand wedge. In a fit of putt pique, he'd broken the designated club over his knee following a particularly gruesome green. The rules say you can't add any clubs (ergo, you shouldn't go breaking any of them) during a round. He'd done the same thing at the TOUR Championship in 1992, but in that case he won the event.

Years ago, the Ladies Professional Golf Association star Jan
Stephenson was given a $4,000 check for acing a hole at an
exhibition in Japan. Too bad her need to reach out and shout
at someone gouged the winnings.

Following the exhibit, she had a transpacific argument
with her boyfriend and spent an hour and 45 minutes on the
phone. Minutes after hanging up, she was handed a phone
bill for $3,200.

"It was a bad decision on my part," Stephenson said.
"Later, I made another bad decision. I married the guy."
The marriage lasted just a bit longer than the phone call.

Bobby Jones might never have been heard of in golf had he
not heeded the sage advice of one of golf's wise men, who told
him he'd never play in a USGA event until he learned to
control his temper.

Twice, Jones, who is remembered as one of golf's scholars and gentlemen, had tossed clubs in anger during competitive play, once striking a woman. The fair warning came from George Walker, great grandfather of President George W. Bush.

From 1923 to 1930, Jones won 13 of the 21 majors he entered. Family, school, job interruptions, and other pressing matters kept him from competing in the 11 other majors for which he was eligible. Using that same yardstick, Tiger Woods is no Bobby Jones. Woods won six of his first 23 majors.

Tom Lehman, one of the Tour's good guys, lists his hobbies in the PGA media guide as hunting and church activities. Still, that doesn't mean he didn't have a devil of a time keeping his temper when it came to golf's frustrations. Lehman broke four clubs over his knee during one round in 1990 when he was still on the Ben Hogan Tour.

Arnold Palmer has given plenty of lessons, but none was as costly as the one he gave Davis Love III at Palmer's 1999 Bay Hill Invitational.

Love, who admits to having less than lovely on-course temper tantrums, hit an errant bunker shot. His next shot, however, was right on target. He clobbered a sprinkler head with his club and sent a gusher of water into the sky. He said he deserved to be fined, and Palmer obliged with a repair bill for $175,003.50 ($3.50 for parts, $175,000 for labor).

Many golfers would happily punch a fist in the air if they ever shot a 75 at Pinehurst during the 1999 U.S. Open. Not Jose Maria Olazabal. He punched a hotel wall.

He said he had kept his emotions in check during the round and later on the practice range and the putting green. In fact, he kept his cool clear up until he got to his hotel room. That's when he took out his fury on the wall.

He didn't have any more temper tantrums during the tournament. That's because he broke the fifth metacarpal bone of his right hand and had to withdraw.

Larry Nelson used three three-iron shots and one four-iron to bogey the par-3 15th hole at the 2002 Senior Players Championship at the TPC of Michigan in Dearborn.

He teed off with a four-iron to the fringe. Next, he used his three-iron to chip it and then he used the same 3-iron to two-putt for a bogey 4. What's so special about the 3-iron? Well, it took the place of the putter he'd bent three holes previously in a fit of rage over his bad putting. "It bent like a rainbow," said Nelson. "Of course, you can't fix it. But I felt like it was a blessing. I ended up putting with my three-iron and shot three under the rest of the way in."

Ace in the Hole

DAVID TOMS SAID the 243-yard hole in one he scored during the third round of the 2001 PGA Championship was "the coolest shot" he'd ever seen. It happened in front of a full gallery. Everybody watching. Nothing fluky. Just right in.

Like Toms, many pros have so many aces they can make distinctions between "good" and "bad" ones. A good ace goes right in; a bad one bounces off a spectator or a rake and rolls in.

What made his hole in one even more cool was that it proved to be the difference in the final outcome of the tournament. He edged Phil Mickelson by one stroke to win the championship. It was the first time someone had made an ace in a major and gone on to win.

Arnold Palmer used a five-iron to ace the 182-yard 3rd hole at the TPC at Avenel during the 1989 Chrysler Cup Pro-Am in Potomac, Maryland.

The next day a TV crew showed up at the hole and told Arnie they were there to film a piece about his hole in one. "You're a day late," Arnie said. "That was yesterday." Arnie, ever the accommodating one, agreed to try to re-create the shot. So he drew out his five-iron, and, while the camera rolled, he aced it again.

Recalled Palmer, "You should have seen the crowd around that hole on the third day. I don't remember what I scored . . . but I know it wasn't another ace."

U.S. Supreme Court Justice Sandra Day O'Connor began golfing while studying law at Stanford University, but didn't take up the game in earnest until 20 years later. Amazingly, she took five years of lessons before ever attempting to stand on a first tee for an actual round.

Then on December 17, 2000, one week after she and her colleagues made a ruling that gave George W. Bush the presidency after the chaotic election of that year, O'Connor got her first ace at the Paradise Valley Country Club in Phoenix.

But she wasn't the first Supreme Court Justice to get an ace. That honor goes to her colleague, John Paul Stevens, who got one in 1990.

Here's one golf record we should all be aiming for: the one held by Harold Stilson, of Deerfield Beach, Florida, who in

2001 at the age of 101 years, 1 month, and 6 days became the oldest golfer ever to get a hole in one when he aced the 108-yard 16th hole at Deerfield Country Club.

Stilson was 71 years old and had already been golfing 50 years when he got his first ace. After that, he was on a comparative tear. The 27 handicapper wound up with six holes in one before passing away in 2002.

One man who was an odds-on favorite to eclipse Stilson was the bionic golfer Barrett Nichols. At 101 he was still swinging in 2002. Nichols, a 23 handicapper, played five times a week at the Meadows Country Club in Sarasota, Florida. From the men's tees (6,028), he shot a 92 at the age of 100, and he was still driving the ball 160 yards.

During spring training in 2001, New York Yankees bench coach Don Zimmer watched his tee shot sail right into the hole at the par-3 12th at Wentworth Golf Club in Tarpon Springs, Florida. It was Zimmer's first ace.

He waved off the advice of his playing partners to retire the ball and hold it for safekeeping. "No way!" he told them. "This ball is bringing me luck!"

Yeah, but it was bad luck. He lost the ball on his very next swing when he dubbed his tee shot straight into a pond. He wound up the day shooting a 135.

Ace in the Hole

It didn't make the papers, and that's a pity because the headline writers would have had a ball with this: "Do You Feel Lucky? Eastwood Sure Does." Or, "Hole in One Makes Eastwood's Day."

Clint Eastwood, one of America's greatest film icons, has been an avid golfer for more than 50 years, yet he never scored an ace until 2001, when his tee shot plunked into the cup on the 7th hole at the lovely Carmel Valley Ranch course near his Carmel-by-the-Sea home.

Referring to a couple of his oft-quoted lines in his Dirty Harry role, Eastwood said the ace made his day and he did feel lucky, too, but for reasons that didn't have anything to do with the ace. When he got to the clubhouse it was deserted, so he didn't have to buy a round of drinks.

Amazing but True Golf Facts

Kim Jong Il, the despotic president of North Korea, shot a jaw-dropping 38-under-par 34 at the Pyongyang Golf Course, in a round that included five aces.

Don't believe it? Well, it was verified by none other than the Pyongyang club pro, Park Young Nam, who said, "Dear Leader comrade general Kim Jong Il, whom I respect from the bottom of my heart, is an excellent golfer."

Of course, the Dear Leader has also been known to violate international nuclear treaties and execute foolhardy dissidents (and, presumably, uncooperatively cranky Pyongyang club pros), so maybe a little scorecard chicanery is not out of the question.

Financial guru Charles Schwab and PGA Tour commissioner Tim Finchem were playing together at a match at Spyglass

Ace in the Hole

Hill. Schwab was up first on a par-3. He hit his ball to within two feet of the flag, a gimme by any standard. Then Finchem whacked his ball straight at the pin. It landed about three feet from the hole and began rolling directly in the path of Schwab's ball. *Boing!* Like a well-executed billiards shot, it struck Schwab's ball and knocked it into the hole for a playing partner–assisted ace.

Alabama golfer Mike Hilyer has 10 aces—incredibly, all of them on par-4s.

In May 2000, *The Golf Journal*, the official publication of the USGA, published an article substantiating nine of them. (The tenth came six months after publication).

None of them came on the same hole or at the same course. All were on holes of at least 300 yards and all were witnessed by sober, independent witnesses.

Amazing but True Golf Facts

One of the aces happened during a tournament on a hole designated for the long-driving competition in which contestants mark their longest drive with a little stake. Hilyer's drive was not only the longest but also the most accurate, landing right in the hole. "I just signed my name on the little card and put the stake in the cup," Hilyer said.

His prize for winning the long-driving competition in such spectacular fashion? A new putter.

Lee Trevino knows it's the little things that count. When he finished the 2001 Par-3 Shootout at the Treetops Resort in Michigan, Trevino judged it a good week because he'd found a dozen balls during the event. Of course, it didn't hurt that he'd won $1.2 million, including a $1 million bonus for scoring a hole in one, the first in the history of the tournament.

Ace in the Hole

Trevino was doubly pleased because $500,000 of the total went to the St. Jude's Children's Hospital in Memphis.

Baseball Hall of Famer Carlton Fisk's dream of getting a hole in one turned into a nightmare, even though the ace he shot at a 1997 pro-am earned him a fabulous Lexus ES300.

He said the IRS took $14,000 right away in taxes, his bar bill was $580, and it cost about $1,200 to ship the car home. "On top of that, I was too big to fit in the car so I had to trade up to something I could squeeze into. That cost another $10,000. So my first lucky ace cost me something like $26,000 for a car I didn't need."

In 1966, New York Yankees legend Joe DiMaggio hosted a tournament at the Sharp Park Golf Course in Pacifica,

California, and donated a color TV set as a prize for anyone who shot a hole in one during the tournament.

Of all the golfers who had a crack at the prize, there was only one whose drive plunked into the cup. The single ace that day came on the 140-yard 15th hole when some lucky guy with an eight-iron knocked one in. The lucky guy? Joe DiMaggio. It's not known whether he accepted the TV that he had donated.

A promise made moments before she hit her tee shot at the 11th hole during the women's 2002 Australian Open cost the American golfer Kelly Robbins more than $50,000.

As she stood on the tee at the 130-yard par-3 hole waiting for the group in front of her to clear the green, Robbins told her caddie, Chuck Parisi, she would give him half of her share of the $212,000 offered as a prize for any golfer who scored an ace on that hole. "I told him I was going to hit it in and that I'd split it with him," she recalled. "I guess you say that often but you never think you are going to do it."

Robbins then put her seven-iron shot directly into the cup for her first hole in one as a professional.

Half of the total prize money for the ace automatically went to the Breast Cancer Research Fund. But Robbins said she would also give away her share. Charities in her hometown of Mount Pleasant, Michigan, would get $53,000 and Parisi would get the other half of her share.

Robbins said she and Parisi had talked about holing out from the tee as they stood waiting to play. Robbins finished the tournament with a three-over 291, yet she actually won more than double the winner, who received $60,000.

Amazing but True Golf Facts

In 1934, Canadian C. Ross (Sandy) Somerville, the first non-American to win the U.S. Amateur two years earlier, became the first golfer to record an ace at the Masters. Somerville aced number 16.

The other par-3s all fell to aces over the years, but the last one didn't fall until 1992. Jeff Sluman became the first golfer ever to ace the 213-yard number 4 hole at Augusta National during the Masters.

In 1959, Patty Berg thrilled the galleries at the U.S. Women's Open at Churchill Valley Country Club by becoming the first woman to record an ace in USGA competition.

It was Berg's first and last ace in a long, prosperous 30-year career of competitive golf.

Ace in the Hole

Years later she recalled what a thrill the shot was for her and how it never bothered her that she didn't get any more after that. "To me, the big thing was I got the first one," she said. "There was only going to be one first and that was all mine. It was a real thrill and I knew it was a shot that would be remembered forever."

In the summer of 1991, at the age of 73, she recorded her second hole in one during a round with friends.

You wouldn't blame the Jubelirer family of Sharon, Pennsylvania, if they put up a shrine at the par-3 9th hole at Squaw Creek Country Club in Vienna, Ohio.

Incredibly, all four members of the family have aced that particular hole.

Mark Jubelirer aced the hole first in 1970. Then mom Natalie got hers in 1993; it was dad Harry's turn in 1997; and finally Mark's brother Steven found the cup in 2001.

Michael Grimaldi, a General Motors sales vice president, nailed a $1 million hole in one at the Indianwood Golf & Country Club in Lake Orion, Michigan, during a charity tournament in 2002.

The only problem was, GM paid Grimaldi's $5,000 entry fee and felt entitled to the prize money. A compromise was reached when GM "allowed" Grimaldi to donate the entire sum to eight charities of his choosing. What, no rebate for the guy who made the shot?

Local pro Stacy Miller left an indelible mark on his ace when his shot literally destroyed the cup.

It happened in 1995 at the par-3, 140-yard 14th hole at Stonehenge Golf Course in Fairfield Glade, Tennessee, which features a spectacular 120-foot vertical drop from tee to green. Miller hit a cloud-kissing nine-iron that sent the ball whistling toward the earth like a laser bomb, landing it one inch in front of the cup. "It's such a steep drop and [the ball] came in so high that it buried into the green and just destroyed the cup." But the ball hit the bottom of the cup for a hole in one.

Ben Hogan has always been known as the game's most obsessive perfectionist—even while sleeping.

He once dreamed of carding an ace on the 1st hole. Then he had aces at the 2nd, 3rd, and 4th holes. In fact, he had scored an ace on each of the first 17 holes. On the 18th hole, he dreamed his shot sailed at the flag, bounced once . . . and lipped out.

Recalled Hogan, "When I woke up, I was mad as hell."

Hot Shots

IN 2002, ANNIKA SORENSTAM arguably had the greatest year of any pro, male or female.

By virtually every category, Sorenstam was the better golfer than Tiger Woods. She won an amazing 47.8 percent of the tournaments she entered, compared to Woods's 27.8 percent; she won 10.3 percent of all the purses while Tiger won 8.2 percent; and her average margin of victory was 3.27 strokes compared to Tiger's 3.00.

To her LPGA competitors, the most frustrating aspect about Sorenstam is that they know no matter what they do physically or mentally to fine-tune their games to compete with her, she's already done it and is probably doing it more tenaciously.

In 2002 she won 13 overall titles and equaled Mickey Wright's record, set back in 1963; she averaged a rarified 68.7 strokes per round, breaking her own record of 69.42, set in 2001; and she earned $2.86 million, another new record that broke another record held by—guess who?—Annika Sorenstam.

Still, when asked what she intended to do in the off-season to prepare for 2003, Sorenstam responded with two words: work harder.

It says something about the vastness of Tiger Woods's golfing achievements that in the 2002 season, in which he won the Masters and the U.S. Open Championship and earned $8 million in competitive revenue, *Golf World* magazine said it was "an average year." But Woods's average is way above average for the rest of the pros.

Unlike Woods, Jack Nicklaus never won 27 tournaments in four years, and Ben Hogan never won four straight Vardon Trophies.

Johnny Miller told *Golf Digest* that Woods is head and shoulders above the greatest golfers who've ever lived. "You look at Bobby Jones, and what he did was amazing," Miller said. "Then you look at Jack Nicklaus, and that was amazing, too. But when you look at Tiger, there's been nothing like it in history."

Craig Perks began 2002 ranked 203rd in the world in a field of fine golfers, many of whom consider The Players Championship at Sawgrass Stadium Course the fifth major.

He played to his ranking by bogeying seven of the first 15 holes in the final round, but still trailed by just one as he walked to the tee at number 16—the first of three ferocious holes that always manage to dash the hopes of numerous contenders. What Perks did next will be remembered at Sawgrass for as long as they play the tournament there.

Perks, who had never played in the Players before, calmly holed a 20-foot chip shot to eagle the 16th. He delighted the crowd at the 17th hole when he staked a nine-iron to 25 feet and drained that putt, too. An aggressive player by nature, Perks didn't back off on the 18th hole, which is annually the toughest on the PGA Tour. From the edge of the green, he chipped in for a miracle par to win the championship with an eight-under 280 and collect $1,800,000.

During his victory speech, he humbly admitted he'd surprised the field and himself. "I hope this isn't my defining moment," he said.

Hot Shots

Dana Quigley may be an old-timer by designation of his status on the Champions Tour (formerly known as the Senior PGA Tour) but he's got the stamina of a boy when it comes to golf. At the age of 55 he set a personal record by playing a remarkable 73 holes in one day in December 2002, at Bear Lakes Country Club, his home course in West Palm Beach, Florida. And he could have gone even more, he says.

"I went sixty holes with my friend Lee Danielian, but he got tired," Quigley said. "Then I played thirteen more. I could have gotten in another twelve after that, but I was going out on a gambling cruise ship that night and had to go home and change."

Quigley, the Cal Ripken of golf, ran his consecutive-start streak to 201 tournaments through 2002 by playing in all 35 Senior tour events. Quigley began his streak in 1997 when he played on a sponsor's exemption at the BankBoston Tournament.

Fred Funk is the PGA Tour's Iron Man, averaging 31.5 tournaments in each of his 14 years on the Tour from 1988 to 2002. The average number played by the top 125 in 2002 was 27, with most of the top players competing in just 18 to 22 events each year.

Funk explained his persistence in a typically workmanlike fashion. "I don't think it's that many," said Funk, who earned a career-high $2,383,071 in 2002. "I play golf for a living. I don't make a living sitting at home. I still enjoy going out to play golf."

For sheer talent, the 1971 class at Tour Qualifying School may have been the best ever. The class included four eventual winners of majors: Tom Watson, John Mahaffey, David Graham, and Lanny Watkins. Other prominent graduates were Leonard Thompson, Bruce Fleisher, and Steve Melnyk.

The former Buy.com Tours might have been the minor leagues, but don't think for a minute that the tournaments were filled with thin fields and poor competition going nowhere.

In 1999, Buy.com alumni won 19 times on the PGA Tour. Because purses were leaner than the fat purses on the big tour, more golfers went for the stick. No wonder guys like David Duval, John Daly, Jim Furyk, and Tom Lehman have thrived on the PGA Tour. They were tested under fire before when they had to win just to survive.

Bob Gilder was never a household name during his days on the PGA Tour, and was often overshadowed by more storied names like Nicklaus, Watson and Miller. But time has a way of rewarding sweet-swinging golfers whose games age gracefully.

Gilder earned top Rookie of the Year honors on the Senior PGA Tour in 2001 when he won twice and had 11 other top-10 finishes. Then, in 2002, he won four times, equaling Tour leader Hale Irwin in victories. Gilder's six wins in two years matched the number of times he won during a 25-year PGA Tour career.

An "eclectic," or "ringer," score occurs when you take the best score you've ever shot on each hole of a particular course that you've played more than once.

The best eclectic score ever may belong to Pat Sutton, former head pro at Riverside Golf Club in Portland, Oregon. Over 58 years, he aced all four par-3s, double-eagled one par-5, and eagled every other hole on the course, for an eclectic score of 35. That's 37 strokes under par.

The amateur golfer Julian Lewis had never had an ace or a double eagle, but on an amazing day in 2002, he got both back-to-back at the Quail Hollow Golf Club in Concord, Ohio.

First, he double-eagled the 490-yard 16th hole. As if that wasn't a remarkable enough feat, he aced the 140-yard, par-3 17th hole.

The day would have been his brother Gary's thirty-sixth birthday, and he thinks his late brother, who'd died tragically the year before, offered a heavenly hand. "When I got the ace, I said, 'Thanks, Gary, I know you must have had something to do with this.'"

Long-driving champion Viktor Johansson routinely hits a golf ball more than 420 yards. His club-head speed has been clocked at 165 mph—most top pros measure out at about 110 miles per hour—and he breaks driver shafts or caves in club heads at least once a week. At long-driving shows he's billed as "Swing Kong."

The 6-foot, 6-inch, 275-pound golfer from Delray Beach, Florida, wows crowds by hitting a ball through a phone book and a ¾-inch piece of plywood. The amazing thing is the ball compresses so much to get through the plywood that it makes a hole actually smaller than the ball itself. A ball can't be passed through the hole.

This passion for power began in 1988 when, at the age of 11, Viktor began playing at a local club in his native country of Sweden. Equally spectacular was his first round of golf, which included an eagle on the course's opening hole.

Jason Bohn, playing in the Canadian pro circuit, set the golf world on fire by shooting a blistering 58 to win the 2001 Bayer Championship at Huron Oaks Golf Club in Sarnia, Ontario. His scorecard included 10 birdies, two eagles, and, yep, a bogey. It could have been a 57.

Bohn's golfing career was financed in 1992 when, as a sophomore at the University of Alabama, he won $1 million after he aced a hole during a local golf tournament. But by accepting the money, he was forced to quit the golf team because of NCAA eligibility requirements.

Still, the money allowed him to pursue his dream of being a professional golfer without the drudgery of earning a living in the meantime, a decision that was very professional by any standard.

After learning that the Pennsylvania club pro Chris Cain had broken his *Guinness Book of Records* world record of playing the most holes in 12 hours, the previous record holder, Brennan Robertson, decided it was time to get serious.

In 1993, when Robertson was 24, he set the world record by playing 456 holes in 12 hours. That mark held until April 2002, when Cain finished 505 holes in the same time frame.

Determined to regain the record, Robertson, director of golf at the Foxfire Golf Club in Sarasota, Florida, hired a personal trainer who could help him with the most demanding part of speed golf: getting in and out of the cart quickly and without getting hurt. His workout consisted of walking, squats and lower body work. He also built up his arms by lifting weights three days a week, full out, and doing a cardio workout five days a week.

In July 2002, aided by a souped-up cart and a NASCAR-like crew, Robertson zoomed though an amazing 535 holes in just 12 hours. He averaged just 81 seconds per hole. With no gimmes!

Anyone looking at amateur golfer Graeme Dawson, who was born without a left arm below the elbow, would think he has a handicap. They would be wrong on two counts.

Playing with a special homemade attachment on his left arm that was approved by the Royal and Ancient Golf Club of St. Andrews, Dawson was listed as a scratch golfer in 2002. He is a former golf team captain at the University of St. Andrews, where he earned undergraduate and advanced degrees in geography.

The strapping 6-footer is capable of driving a ball 300 yards, has the course record of 62 at his old home course, Ranfurly Castle, near Glasgow, and shot a 68 from the back tees at Shinnecock Hills.

One of the greatest streaks in golf is in the firm, able hands of 73-year-old Betty Dunham.

In 2002, she won her nineteenth Onawa (Iowa) Country Club women's championship. What makes the record so remarkable is that it spans six decades. Betty has won championships in the 1950s, 1960s, 1970s, 1980s, 1990s and in the first decade of 2000.

Many amateur golfers say that after getting a hole in one, it's hard to shoot well because they are so pumped.

If that's true, it's a wonder Tom Doty didn't spontaneously combust during an amazing round in October 1971 at an executive course near his Chicago home.

After birdieing the first hole, he nailed back-to-back aces and then recorded another birdie. Unfortunately, we don't know what he shot for the rest of the day. Perhaps he did spontaneously combust. For four holes he certainly was on fire.

Judy Eller Street was a junior at the University of Miami in 1959 when she won the national golf championship for women. Like many female golfers and athletes of the time, she dropped out to marry and have a family.

What's unusual is the way she dropped back in.

After her marriage broke up in the mid-nineties, she decided to go back to college at Barry University in Miami Shores, Florida. While attending a school banquet, the women's basketball coach, Jan Allen, heard Judy's story and her background. "Wouldn't it be funny if Judy had another year's eligibility and could play golf here?" Allen told school officials. (College athletes have four years of eligibility)

After some quick checking, it was determined Judy did have a year remaining. So, at the age of 62, Judy became the number 3 player on the team, helping it reach sixth in the NCAA Division II rankings in 2002. Judy is believed to be the oldest NCAA athlete ever.

Elimination was the inspiration for the University of Minnesota Golden Gopher golfers.

The sport had been a fixture on campus for 88 years when Coach Brad James was told that for financial reasons the school would no longer support the golf program and that 2002 would be the golfing Gophers' last season.

The university was quitting on the team, but the team wasn't about to quit. Just 57 days after being informed that the school planned to drop the program, teammates Matt Anderson, Simon Nash, Wilhelm Schauman, David Morgan, and Justin Smith won the NCAA golf title. With their achievement they earned the team a stay of execution.

"Golf was the only thing we could control," said Coach James. He used the trophy to raise $2.7 million to fund the golf team through 2005. "That tends to open people's wallets."

There's no limit to the heights that golfer Lorena Ochoa could reach—on and off the course.

In 2002 when she was a 21-year-old sophomore at the University of Arizona, the native of Guadalajara, Mexico, set the standard for female collegiate golfers, winning a remarkable seven straight events and 8 of 10 total tournaments. She turned pro that same year and won three Futures Tour events and the Tour's money title.

A noted outdoorswoman, she isn't discouraged by a layout with a lot of breaks. After competing in a tournament in Japan in 2002, she left the locker room and climbed Mount Fuji.

Frank McCarthy, 68, of Silver Spring, Maryland, not only shot his age at nearby Argyle Country Club in 2002, but he did it in style. His 68 included an amazing eight consecutive birdies on holes 8 through 15.

Of the streak McCarthy said, "I was thinking it was going to be over after each hole. We [his foursome] were pretty quiet until the 13th hole, when I rolled in a thirty-five-foot putt from just off the backside of the green. At that point I just laughed. Then we all did. It was a once-in-a-lifetime round."

Mark Boe wasn't going to let torn ligaments stop him from competing with his teammates at Waikato High School in New Zealand in 2002. With his right arm in a sling, Boe, 17, used his good left arm to win not one but two matches against a rival high school. He said, only half jokingly, that the results had him thinking about playing one-handed all the time.

It was a team match, but no one could dispute that Boe beat the rivals single-handedly.

Amazing but True Golf Facts

A thirteen-year-old Korean boy, Jae An, is the youngest male to qualify for a professional golf tournament and the youngest to make the cut. An played in the New Zealand Open in January 2001. His father carried his bag. The solidly built An, who plays to a handicap of one, moved with his family to New Zealand in 1999.

Inside the Ropes

LEE JANZEN ALWAYS KEEPS THREE COINS in his pocket to use as markers on the putting greens.

He uses the quarter for long putts, the nickel for medium putts, and the dime for wee ones. The years on the coins don't matter to him, but since September 11, 2001, Janzen always takes care to make sure one aspect of his coin selection is always the same. He puts a New York quarter, depicting the Statue of Liberty, in his pocket to remember those who lost their lives that day.

For as long as he's played competitive golf, Jack Nicklaus has always carried three pennies in his pocket for marking purposes.

Why three? "Years ago, an incident made me think that if I carried just one penny and lost it, I'd be without a ball marker. If I carried two, lost one, and a fellow competitor needed one, I'd again be without a marker. So it's three pennies for me. One more thing: I always mark with the tail side up."

Besides seeing their names high on the leader board, Tour players say they enjoy looking at the beautiful nannies Jesper Parnevik has hired to watch his children. In several published polls among players, Jesper's kids' nannies were named as the most beautiful wives/girlfriends/women on the Tour.

Like many of the Tour participants, Tiger Woods had his eye on one of the nannies, and in 2002 he began dating the Swedish beauty, Elin Nordegren. Parnevik introduced the nanny, who sometimes modeled on the side, to Woods. It wasn't long before Tiger and Elin were an item, causing Jesper to feign chagrin.

"The original plan was to get Tiger distracted," Jesper said. "But it hasn't seemed to work."

Mark Calcavecchia says the look of grim determination on his face as he marches up and down the fairways is not indicative of the kind of guy he is.

He is, he says, a happy guy, someone who enjoys life. It's just that earning a living playing golf is different from simply playing golf. And it shows. "I'm the happiest guy in the world nineteen hours a day. It's the five hours I'm out on the golf course that I'm miserable. But that's not bad when you're happy most of the day."

Greg Norman has endured his share of sinking feelings on the golf course. Let's hope it never happens on the high seas. Norman took receipt of a 285-foot yacht in 2003, the $70 million *Aussie Rules*, the largest aluminum motor yacht in the world. The vessel took 300 workers three years to construct and features seven auxiliary boats and a tackle room for 200 fishing rods.

In 2002 Tiger Woods's mom, Kultilda, gave her son a headcover shaped like a tiger's head. What appears to be strange lettering to most American golf fans was something Woods recognized right away. On it she stitched a message in Thai (which he can read). It says: "Love from Mom."

With a name like Charles Howell III, it wouldn't do to dress like Joe Six-pack.

So Howell is under contract to wear exclusively clothes made by Johan Lindeberg, a cutting-edge Swedish designer whose clothes got Jesper Parnevik nicknamed "The Pink Panther" for wearing them.

Howell says the best way to distinguish oneself on the golf course is to play well, but it doesn't hurt to dress well. "You want to be different, but still be classy," Howell says. "I don't want to see a picture of myself fifteen years from now looking like an idiot."

It may be too late for that, according to some observers. At the 2002 Masters he wore pants with a single stripe down each leg. "The first person to see me in them was Tiger Woods, and he gave me a really funny look."

Phil Mickelson is probably tired of hearing about it, but so were Doug Sanders, Harry Cooper, Bruce Crampton, and Macdonald Smith. Those were the PGA Tour players who had gotten the most top-three finishes in a major without winning one.

At the start of the 2003 season, Mickelson led the list with seven in that category compared with six apiece for Sanders and Cooper, and five each for Crampton and Smith.

Billy Casper had tried elk, hippo, and other exotic meats before settling on the one delicacy that he said helped him win 51 PGA Tour events, including a Masters and two U.S. Open titles.

Need a hint? Casper's nickname became Buffalo Bill. Yep, it was eating buffalo that he said helped him consume the competition. It's a good thing, too, at least for the sake of his nickname. It wouldn't do to call a golf champion something like Kangaroo Casper.

John Daly has been called the Elvis of golf, and it's not hard to see why.

His larger-than-life persona has made him a fan favorite. His $1.4 million Prevost customized motor home can go about 85 mph and gets 6 miles to the gallon. He parks it outside his 11,000-square-foot Dardanelle, Arkansas, home. The walls in the house are adorned with 130 signed football jerseys, and there are 47 guitars on display. The big boy is living large.

Jim Thorpe lost his Tour card in 1987 after blowing out his wrist trying to hit a shot off a tree root. He was 42 and had earned $1.9 million. He was never able to recover his form on the PGA Tour.

He waited until he became eligible for the Senior PGA Tour in 1999 and then went on a tear, earning $4.3 million through the 2002 season.

Thorpe, who came from a family of 12, says he remembers growing up poor. "When you're broke you can't get a break. My daddy would be amazed that in one year I made $1.8 million. He wouldn't believe it."

Phil Mickelson blamed some bad putting in 2002 on neglecting his practice.

He said he used to be golden on three-footers because of a drill he did in which he wouldn't leave the putting green until he made 100 three-footers in a row. "I didn't miss a three-footer for months." But once he began skipping the drill, he began missing a few three-footers.

The drill was a technique he learned from Jackie Burke, a PGA Hall of Famer, for whom it was a religion during his PGA heyday.

Several years ago, Burke bet Mickelson a dinner at a fancy restaurant near Houston that Mickelson couldn't make 100 in a row. Mickelson wanted to double the bet. "I can't eat that much," Burke said. Mickelson missed his third attempt and lost the bet. But he gained a valuable practice technique that seldom fails him—unless he fails to do the drill.

LPGA star Cristie Kerr really loved hitting the road on Tour, where her life was in marked contrast to the boot-camp conditions of her home life.

On tour, she stays in the finest hotels, eats the best meals, and is waited on by fawning staff who are on hand to see to her every needs. However, home for her in 2002 was a modest apartment she shared with fiancé Captain Robb Sucher of the U.S. Marine Corps. They lived on base at Twentynine Palms, California.

After decades-long speculation, Ben Hogan's much-rumored "secret" remains just that.

In 1953, *Golf Digest* suggested it was a 20-minute swing regimen he performed each morning. *Life* magazine later quoted experts who theorized it was a number of precise technical adjustments. It may have been that his secret was one we all know and rarely practice. In fact, Hogan's secret may have been just that—practice, practice, practice.

Phil Mickelson's father, Phil Sr., would always whisper in young Phil's ear before a tournament, "Go out and have fun." But in the other ear his mother, Mary, would whisper a more competitive message: "Have fun, but be sure to win."

In 2001 when she was 59, the 5-foot-8-inch Mary Mickelson played guard on a basketball team that won the three-on-three gold medal for the 50-and-over teams at the Senior Olympics. Some days she and her son can be found at the local YMCA playing two-on-two basketball, and beating some smart-aleck high schoolers.

Golf writer John Huggan had a tough time getting anyone to say anything nice about his subject when he told fellow golfers he was doing a profile on Nick Faldo.

One player even reached out, snapped off the tape recorder, and proceeded to call Faldo every bad name in the book.

Faldo was trying to undergo a public transformation where he was being kinder to the media and more open about himself. But it wasn't impressing Mark Calcavecchia. "He's the same guy he's always been," Calc said. "He may come off as more affable to the press, but when he's out playing, he still doesn't say [anything]. Playing with Nick Faldo is like playing by yourself . . . only slower."

Ben Crenshaw has such a love for the history of golf that he convinced his wife, Julie, to name their cats after famous golfers. During their years together, they've had cats named Francis Ouimet, Ben Hogan, and Bobby Jones.

Bruce Lietzke dreams of the day when thousands of people are watching his every move and screaming the name "Bruce! Bruuuce! Bruuuuce!"

But it's not him in the dream, and the screaming isn't taking place around the 18th green of some championship course. No, Lietzke says he wishes he could be Bruce Springsteen for a day. "In my real life, I'm a professional golfer, but in my dream life, I'm a rock star in front of millions and millions of people. I couldn't possibly do it in my real life, but Bruce Springsteen is probably my favorite rock musician. I like his music and the way he handles himself on stage. I would dream to be that."

The year 2002 could be remembered as the season of awkward celebrations.

First it was Rich Beem's hip-wiggling tribute to lack of rhythm after he sank the final putt to win the 2002 PGA Championship at Hazeltine.

Then came Paul Azinger's awkward attempts to celebrate his remarkable bunker shot on the 18th hole at The Belfry during the Ryder Cup singles matches. After holing the 25-foot miracle sand shot to halve his match with Niclas Fasth and give the U.S. team a flicker of hope, Azinger jumped out of the bunker and tried to high-five his caddie four times, each time missing his outstretched hand.

Some golfers, as Azinger and Beem proved, ought to stick to just politely tipping their caps.

In high school, Cristie Kerr was overweight, wore glasses, and was teased by some of her classmates.

She found solace—and redemption on the golf course. She eventually dropped 50 pounds and joined the LPGA. Today the 5-foot-4-inch, 125-pound blonde has been described in sex-symbol terms by *Golf* magazine. In 2002, she had a breakout year with a Tour victory and stirring play in the 2002 Solheim Cup matches in which the United States beat the Europeans. She finished twelfth on the year's money list.

You can bet Kerr's looking forward to those high school reunions.

A few years after turning pro, Tiger Woods was asked by a reporter what he remembered most about his rookie year on the Tour.

The writer expected Woods to talk about his runaway 12-stroke victory at the Masters in 1997, chatting with Oprah, or posing with showgirls. Woods, who was just 20 years old in his rookie season, said the most impressive part of the Tour was receiving all the gifts and perks lavished on the players. Said Woods, "Getting all the free stuff. Man, that was great."

Inside the Ropes

Fuzzy Zoeller is known as a fast-talking, fun-loving hustler, but he's as competitive as anyone when it comes to golf. Still, he says there's one match he didn't mind losing.

It was to his youngest daughter, Gretchen, who was 18. She was a four handicapper and beat her old man from the men's tees (he was playing from the pro tees) at their hometown course in Floyds Knobs, Indiana. "I thought it was the greatest thing in the world," Fuzzy said.

In the old days of golf, any discussion of physical fitness began and ended with Gary Player. He ate garlic to boost his immune system, lifted weights to strengthen his muscles, and ran laps to improve his endurance. He said he did so to compete with the likes of Arnold Palmer and Jack Nicklaus, men he considered stronger and more talented than himself.

Nowadays, it's hard to find a player on the Tour who does not work out, and for many the fitness trailer has become as important a stop as the driving range. Still, too rigorous a training routine can be harmful. David Duval admits that he became such a fitness fanatic that he suffered workout-related injuries that hurt his golf. In 2002, while nursing his injuries, he finished eightieth on the money list.

Some people react with restraint when accepting august awards such as induction into the World Golf Hall of Fame. Both Judy Rankin and Juli Inkster gave speeches so joyous that they were overcome by the moment and wept openly over the plaudits that came their way during induction ceremonies in 2001.

Tart-tongued Jackie Burke, winner of the 1956 Masters and PGA Championship, reacted a bit differently to his induction. When it was his turn to follow Inkster and Rankin, he broke up the crowd when he looked at the tear-stained faces of the two LPGA players and said, "Girls, you've got me in casual water up here."

Strong drink has hurt the games of many PGA Tour pros over the years, none more so than David Frost's. But not in the way you might think.

The 10-time Tour winner is an accomplished vintner who grew up on a vineyard in the Stellenbosch region of South Africa and still practices his winemaking art. "It has hurt my game a little bit," said Frost, who in 2002 finished 126th on the money list. "But I'm not just lending my name to wine-making. For me, it's the family business."

Amazing but True Golf Facts

Tiger Woods and other top Tour pros don't have to worry about getting a house sitter to grab the mail, water the plants, and make sure the dog gets walked. Woods has personal assistants who take care of the house, and IMG sports management takes care of paying his bills.

Woods doesn't waste time being placed on hold to wait for airline reservations. When he wants to play in a tournament, he tells IMG associates, who order a charter jet and tell Woods when the plane will be ready. They also make his hotel reservations and take care of other travel needs.

Tour pro Dudley Hart conceived a way to ensure a large and supportive gallery whenever he shows up at the first tee. He and his wife, Suzanne, had triplets—Ryan, Abigail, and Rachel—on December 6, 2001.

Even though it's a costly enterprise, the Harts try to ensure that the whole family, plus at least one nanny, make the trip to many of the Tour stops where Hart competes. "It's great for me to have my family there," Dudley says. "To go even two weeks without seeing the kids is really tough. Their personalities are coming out now. They grab onto you and smile when you come home. They walk like I did in college after a long night."

It took a little wifely heckling for Joe Durant to get his game in order. After nearly quitting golf in 1991 to sell insurance and work in a golf warehouse, Durant began playing professional golf again, and doing it very well. Still, he wasn't satisfied with his performance, even though he was regularly shooting 67 or 68.

"I was still complaining about it," he said. "My wife said, 'Look, if you do not go out with a better attitude, we're not going to do this.' She knew I was being a wimp, basically. Nobody wants to hear a complainer, and she wasn't going to put up with it."

From 1997, when he joined the Tour, through 2002, he earned more than $4.4 million.

◉

Vijay Singh celebrated his fortieth birthday in 2003 by giving himself an addition that will help ensure no additions to his silhouette. Singh added a gymnasium to his house, equipped with 20 new fitness machines to help him keep in shape.

◉

When Rich Beem won his first Tour victory at the 1999 Kemper Open, he looked nervous as he sat down before the assembled media. He then explained why: "This is different.

I'm used to sitting around and saying bad things about my round."

The nickname "the Golden Bear" came from an Australian golf writer, Don Lawrence, who in 1963 overheard Jack Nicklaus's agent, Mark McCormack, refer to Jack as a "golden bear."

The next day Lawrence started referring to the then jumbo-sized Jack as a golden bear of a golfer. The image fit the big Ohio golfer with the Midas touch, and soon golf writers all over the United States began picking up on it. Coincidentally, Nicklaus was a golden bear long before the Aussie writer dubbed him one. His high school mascot was also a golden bear.

The European golfer Pierre Fulke gave Sam Torrance a frightful moment when he called to inform Torrance, the captain of the 2003 European Ryder Cup team, that he was in dire straits.

Torrance had just stepped out of the shower in his hotel room when Fulke called. Recalled Torrance, "He says, 'Sam, I've got a huge problem. It's the biggest problem of the week. I have to come see you.' So I wrap a towel around myself and go to the door and his face is ashen. I thought, 'What has happened?' He says, 'Sam, I can't do my tie.' I could have killed him." Instead, still dripping from his shower, the captain helped Fulke tie his tie.

The death of Sam Snead in 2002 brought many tributes to the sweetest swinger the game's ever known.

Snead was so athletic and limber that late into his life he could still impress golfers who were decades younger than him by kicking the top of a door jamb from a standing position.

Still, for golf purposes, many were even more impressed by what Snead carried and played in his bag until the day he died. One admirer, Nick Faldo, marveled that Snead still kept a one-iron in his bag at the age of 89. "There won't be too many people who can do that," Faldo said.

Jesper Parnevik is the New Age king of the golf world.

He eats volcanic sand and fruit to cleanse his system. He says he's manipulated his blood magnetism and aura (supposedly that's a good thing) and sometimes wears glasses with flashing lights designed to synchronize his right and left brains (supposedly that's a good thing too). He's tried ESP,

retinal readings, crystals, and various bearded gurus—all in the
hope of getting an edge.

Billy Dunk may be the greatest pro you've never heard of.
In the 1960s and '70s, Dunk won more than 100 Australian
tournaments, including five Australian PGA championships.
He broke a whopping 80 course records.

    Many of the pros and sportswriters were buzzing about how
well Dunk would do when he made the long flight above the
equator to play against the best players on the PGA Tour. But
it never happened. Sure, he could have been a sensation on
the international scene, but he never tried—because he didn't
like to fly.

Champions Tour player Jim Thorpe is a big man with XXL hands that can crush bones when he gives you a friendly squeeze. Try this: See how many golf balls you can pick up with one hand. Most golfers have trouble pawing more than five. Thorpe's mitt can grasp an amazing eight.

Jim was the ninth of 12 children and big hands helped him survive the nightly competition to grab some food at the dinner table before it was all gone.

Tiger Woods says he eats to win.

Before tournaments he consumes green vegetables, fruit and fruit juices, turkey, baked fish, grilled chicken, skimmed milk, egg whites, and rice, which he says keep his body in a winning form.

He says he avoids certain foods that he believes can make him lose. He never consumes pizza, ice cream, cheesecake, roast beef, fried chicken and fish, gravy, ham, or soft drinks before a round.

"I still love the occasional cheeseburger and I'm a sucker for Mom's sticky rice and mangoes, but I no longer pig out on them," he says. "My goal is to remain healthy my entire career, and a healthy diet seems like a good start."

Tom Lehman said he never knew he had what it took to make it as a pro until he hit an eight-iron approach on the 72nd hole of the PGA Tour Qualifying School in 1990 when he needed a birdie to go on or go home. He put the pressure shot three feet from the cup and sank it.

Lehman had first turned pro in 1982 but lost his card in 1987 after winning only $40,000 in five years. It took him another three years and a Q-school shot before he figured he belonged.

He earned over $12 million during the next ten years on the tour. He credits, besides that confidence-boosting shot, his wife, Melissa, with giving him focus to do well on the Tour.

In fact, he even enlisted Melissa to caddie for him at the 1998 Nissan Open when his regular caddie, Andy Martinez, suffered two broken ribs in a pickup basketball game the night before the first round. Lehman shot a two-over 286.

Michael and Linda Kerr chose their daughter Cristie's path in life early on. When Cristie was 14, her father ordered a license plate that read "LPGA 96," for the year he prophesied his daughter would turn pro.

After becoming the low amateur at the 1996 U.S. Women's Open, Cristie proved her father's prediction right. She qualified for the LPGA Tour at the age of 19 in 1996. By the end of the 2000 season, she was ranked fifteenth in earnings.

Many golfers fortunate enough to have enjoyed the thrill of winning the British Open keep the prize—the venerable Claret Jug—locked away. Not David Duval.

When he won at the Royal Lytham and St. Anne's in 2001 with a 10-under 274, he took the trophy and set it on the counter at the pro shop at Pablo Creek Golf Club, his home course near Jacksonville, Florida. "I certainly wasn't going to carry it around with me," he explained. "I felt I would leave it at home [the local golf club] so people can enjoy it."

Inside the Ropes

It takes a pretty special athlete to wrest the Canadian Athlete of the Year honor away from a hockey player in hockey-mad Canada, but Tour player Mike Weir was named Canadian Male Athlete of Year not once but twice, in 2000 and 2001.

Still, Weir idolizes the guys on the frozen pond. He skipped both the Buick Invitational and the Nissan Open to watch Team Canada and his Canuck buddy Mario Lemieux skate their way to Olympic gold in 2002. He went on to win the Masters in 2003.

Flak and Fuss

WHEN HOOTIE JOHNSON TANGLED with Martha Burk, the head of the National Council of Women's Organizations, over the club's male-only membership, he vowed that Augusta National would never "become a trophy in her display case." It had apparently been a while since he'd peeked in his own display case. Martha Burk already managed to get a trophy of hers into the sacred area in an odd sort of way.

Among the memorabilia in the Augusta National club-house is a putter once used by Bobby Jones, which he called "Calamity Jane" after the famous nineteenth-century heroine of the wild, wild West. The real Calamity Jane was born

Flak and Fuss

Martha Cannary in 1852. In 1885 she married a man named Clinton Burk. That made her married name . . . Martha Burk.

Golf gets itself into trouble whenever it tries to incorporate NFL-style promotions and gimmicks into its pastoral settings. That's what happened at the 2002 Target World Challenge in Thousand Oaks, California, where organizers thought it would be a good idea to arrange a military flyover by four jet fighter planes.

The jets buzzed above the Sherwood Country Club as players and fans paused in admiration of the military might. But the excitement proved too much for a couple of Arabian horses in a nearby stable. The noise frightened them so badly they panicked, injured themselves, and, sadly, died.

Both the horses and the course were owned by a multi-millionaire, David Murdock, who was reportedly furious over the deaths.

Lee Trevino knows a thing or two about fistfights, the 62-year-old told *Golf Digest*. He said his last fight occurred in 1978, after he'd won a $200 bet with the then mayor of El Paso, Texas. The two had bet on who was the winner of the last El Paso Open back in 1959. The mayor said it was one of the Hebert brothers, while Trevino said it was Marty Furgol. Trevino was right.

Recalled Trevino, "When I came to collect, a TV crew was waiting there, and here came the mayor with a huge bag of pennies, one hundred dollars' worth. He poured the bag of pennies over my head, which I didn't think was one bit funny."

Trevino warned the mayor not to pour the other bag over his head, but the warning was ignored. "He just laughed and started to pour anyway, so I cold-cocked him. When they showed me punching out the mayor on TV, I got a lot of phone calls, all of them congratulating me. People didn't like that mayor."

The Ryder Cup used to be a gentle, fun get-together, where the wives of American and European golfers shopped together, players dined together, and the fans applauded for players from both sides of the ocean. What happened to change that chumminess? European golfers got good.

The United States had held the Cup an amazing 20 out of 21 times from 1935 to 1983. In the mid-eighties, the Ryder Cup became extremely competitive and, thus, contentious— and ever since there has been a tremendous Ry-valry.

The originator of the tournament, golf philanthropist Samuel Ryder, might be ashamed of the bitter spectacle that sometimes erupts at his namesake tournament. In 1926, he said of his idea: "Why can't they all get to know one another? They can play some matches and have a party afterward—with champagne and chicken sandwiches."

Catrin Nilsmark, an LPGA Tour player, caused a stir at the Asahi Tyokuken International Championship in North Augusta, South Carolina, in 2001 when the leggy former runway model showed up wearing short shorts.

Many of the men simply admired her legs, some of the women were more critical of her attention-drawing drawers, but one competitor had a more practical question. Of the

5-foot-11 Nilsmark and her short shorts one player remarked, "I just wonder: Where does she put her tees?"

Nilsmark says she wears the shorts for the most basic of reasons: they feel good. She even says they're a bit baggy. "I like them, other people seem to like them. Honestly, there's even enough room in my back pocket for a spare ball and my scorecard."

If there's any doubt as to the clout that Tiger Woods has, his caddie, Steve Williams, can set the record straight.

Williams was on the bag for Woods at the made-for-TV *Showdown at Sherwood* in 1999 on a stifling hot evening in late August, near Los Angeles. Officials told the caddie he had to wear long pants, a decision that angered Williams. "I thought that was ridiculous. It was real hot," he recalled. According to Williams, here's what happened next:

A PGA Tour official went up to Woods and said, "If your caddie doesn't put on pants, you aren't playing."

So Tiger said, "Then I'm not playing."

The official said, "If you aren't playing here, then you aren't playing the PGA Tour."

Tiger replied, "Good. I'll go play in Europe."

Tiger played . . . and Williams wore shorts.

The rascals at *Playboy* magazine stirred up a hornets' nest of publicity for the LPGA Tour in 2002 when they asked for, and received, headshots of nine players to enter into an on-line poll in which viewers would pick the LPGA's sexiest golfer. The "prize" would be a photo feature in the magazine.

The winner was Carin Koch. However, she declined a six-figure sum to doff her duds and reveal herself for *Playboy* readers; so did the runner-up, Jill McGill, but not without giving the idea some consideration. "I'm not saying no, but if I say yes, I might have to do a few more situps," McGill said.

What generated even more sexy buzz for the LPGA was an unintentionally provocative photo taken of Cristie Kerr kissing the crystal phallus-like trophy after her 2002 victory at Longs Drugs Challenge. Kerr went on to record eight top-10 finishes and moved from twenty-eigth to twelfth on the money list to keep reminding the public of her golfing abilities, but the racy picture will be provoking chuckles as long as there's an Internet.

Sergio Garcia's animated antics at the 2002 Ryder Cup didn't just get on the nerves of his opponents. It was upsetting to the guys who carried their clubs, too.

Not only would he react with overzealous joy at making gimme putts, but he'd throw tantrums when falling short, once kicking his bag and driver up and down a fairway in an unseemly fit that provoked many strong reactions—few of them supportive of the 22-year-old Garcia.

John Burke, Davis Love III's caddie, fumed, "He doesn't win with class and he doesn't lose with class."

Flak and Fuss

While the 2002 Ryder Cup at The Belfry, in Sutton Coldfield, England, captained by Sam Torrance for the European team and Curtis Strange for the American, was a model of sportsmanlike comportment, the 2002 Solheim Cup at Interlachen Country Club in Edina, Minnesota, could have used some United Nations monitors to fend off hostilities.

The Swedish player Catrin Nilsmark spent each press conference spewing nasty remarks about her U.S. counterparts. On a Swedish website she called Cristie Kerr "a little brat" and said Michele Redman had "a complete lack of talent."

The U.S. team politely refused to be drawn in, claimed to be amused . . . and then went out and whipped Nilsmark and her team by three points.

Much was made of it when golf's elder statesmen came out and criticized today's Tour players for being too sheepish to beat

Tiger Woods. One of the pros singled out by Arnold Palmer and Jack Nicklaus was Phil Mickelson.

But Mickelson fired back with one of his best shots ever, one that must have scorched the Golden Bear. Said Mickelson: "When Nicklaus used to win majors, he would kind of hang in there, hang in there, and guys would come back and hand it to him. If he took that attitude now, I don't think he'd win any because Tiger is not making those mistakes."

The problem is that Mickelson usually does.

John Cook took the time to stir the pot, too. "Tiger would beat the brains out of all those guys. He and Jack would be a great duel every week, but I'll take Phil [Mickelson], Ernie [Els] and Retief [Goosen] against [Lee] Trevino, [Arnold] Palmer and [Billy] Casper."

Flak and Fuss

It may not have garnered as much publicity, but the policy that provoked the greater sting at Augusta National was not about admitting women members. No, it was Hootie Johnson's decision to impose an age limit of 65 (and a 10-event minimum) on Masters competitors that rankled many in the golf community. Johnson coldly informed numerous past champions of his decision by letter.

The decision applied to past champions like Gay Brewer, Billy Casper, and Gary Player, and perhaps even Jack Nicklaus would be forbidden from playing the most hallowed tournament in golf. Nicklaus said, "You're usually hurt by the things you love the most. I love the Masters a lot."

The letter also contributed to a decision by Arnold Palmer, who more than any other man made the Masters a popular event, to announce that the 2002 tournament would be his last Masters. "I don't want to get a letter," Palmer said.

Palmer's comment caused such a backlash that Augusta's new policy allows players to compete as long as they feel they can play competively.

The green jackets awarded to Masters champions aren't supposed to leave the grounds and are even dry-cleaned at Augusta National.

Gary Player, winner of the Masters in 1961, 1974, and 1978, got in trouble for taking one of his home to South Africa. When Masters founder Clifford Roberts asked for its return, Player reportedly told him, "You'll have to come get it if you want it back."

But as a concession, Player agreed never to wear his jacket, and he never has—not even to dinner at his own house. It just hangs there in his closet (or so he says).

Was there some cheating at the 1999 Ryder Cup?

Ricci Roberts, caddie for Europe's Andrew Coltart, claims there was chicanery during a pivotal match against Tiger Woods on the final day of competition at the Country Club in Brookline, Massachusetts. Ricci swears that after Coltart sent an errant shot deep into the woods, a marshal stood on Coltart's ball for five minutes until time expired, forcing the player to take a penalty and drop.

After Coltart had been penalized and had taken his next shot, the marshal said, "Here's a Titleist with a blue dot on it." It was Coltart's ball. Roberts said the ball was imbedded in the ground—with a deep shoeprint around it.

Woods won the match . . . and the United States won the Cup by one point.

Many golfers expressed consternation that both the European Tour's 2002 Volvo Masters and the 2002 Australian PGA Championships ended in ties because the leaders didn't want to play anymore.

At Spain's Valderrama Golf Course, Bernhard Langer and Colin Montgomerie finished 72 rounds at 281 and agreed to split a purse of more than $800,000 rather than engage in a sudden-death playoff the following day. In the Australian tournament, coleaders Peter Lonard and Jarrod Moseley decided not to continue their Sunday battle into Monday and divided the million-dollar first-place prize.

Having cochampions who chose not to continue sudden-death playoffs caused some pros to question the winners' competitive spirit. Tiger Woods wondered, "Whose picture do they put on the program next year?"

Flak and Fuss

The Tour today is so rife with big money that many pros will opt out of a champion-determining playoff in order to fly to the next big money payday, content with the winnings they've earned from half a victory.

A New Zealand golf web site that carried details on the time and date of every round played by all registered golfers in the country was closed down in 2001 when players complained that their bosses were finding out that they'd been out golfing when they were supposed to be in the office or at business meetings.

Head Games

JACK NICKLAUS MAY LOOK like he has nerves of steel, but even the Golden Bear gets first-tee jitters, and that can lead to short, fast swings and poor starts.

To prevent this, Nicklaus has developed his own soothing mantra. He recites in his mind, "Complete the backswing." The cue helps him concentrate on swinging his left shoulder under his chin before he starts the crucial downswing on the first hole.

How tough is golf? It makes even the best in the game feel like losers.

Head Games

Two days after winning his second U.S. Open in 1997 at the Congressional Country Club, Ernie Els was telling reporters that everyone in golf winds up a loser. "The game gives you more downs than ups. I'm in my fourth year as a professional and I've probably played in sixty tournaments. Yet, I've won just five times. Only five. That's not very good, even though I'm considered one of the best in the game. Golf is a tough game and it's going to make losers out of all of us."

Sports psychologist Bob Rotella has been asked to interpret his share of golf dreams, but the one he has never gotten over is the one Donna Caponi had on the evening before she won the 1969 U.S. Women's Open.

Caponi said that she dreamed she was walking down the final fairway on the last day of the U.S. Open. When she got to the ball, she was dismayed to see that it was in a deep divot.

"She said she swings, and the ball pops straight up and comes down in the same divot, which is now deeper," Rotella recalled. "She swings again, same thing. She keeps flailing away and she's in a trench. At that point she woke up in a cold sweat."

The next day, the final day of the Open, Caponi hit a drive on the 18th tee, and from a distance she could see that it had landed in a divot, just like the dream. But when she got to the ball she saw it was in a very shallow divot.

Said Rotella, "She was so relieved she thought nothing of it, and birdied the hole to win the first of her two Opens."

Veteran Tour player Mark O'Meara has acknowledged that he took on a mentoring role to his younger neighbor, Tiger Woods, when Woods moved to Windermere, Florida, shortly after joining the Tour.

But O'Meara admits that he got more out of the relationship than Woods did.

Without playing against Tiger Woods on a near-daily basis, O'Meara figures he never would have won his first two majors—the 1998 Masters and the 1998 British Open. He said playing with and against Tiger sharpened his game in ways that days on the Tour against top players never could.

The top players were good, but they just weren't Tiger—and for O'Meara that made all the difference.

John Restino was near the bottom of the rankings at 115 on the Buy.com Tour money list when his sponsor called up with some distressing news. The sponsor said it was time maybe Restino started looking for a new line of work.

The next week, Restino finished in a four-way tie for first place at the 2002 State Farm Open, losing out in a playoff to

Andy Miller. Restino admitted that the sponsor's threat was a wake-up call. That kind of pressure is inspirational to golfers who are faced with going up in the standings or going home to a real job. Restino finished the year ranked sixty-eighth.

The few pros who've ever broken 60 have said they were "in the zone"—a mental state in which they were so focused they blocked out distractions and hit their shots to spots exactly where they had visualized them moments earlier.

At the Buy.com Tour's 1998 Miami Valley Open, Doug Dunakey was in "the zone." When he reached the 18th green, he needed to make a 25-foot putt to shoot what would be a record-shattering 57. As he studied his lie, dozens of his fellow pros were scrambling to the 18th green to watch him make history. Unfortunately, the flurry of activity around the green broke Dunakey's concentration. He ended up three-putting, which was still good enough for an amazing 59, equaling the record for the best 18-hole score on the pro circuit.

Ernie Els won the 2003 Sony Open after a second-hole playoff win over Aaron Baddeley, but Els admitted that a coin nearly cost him the tournament.

On the 17th hole, Baddeley, who has played in Europe and in Australia, marked his 3-foot putt with an English one-pound sterlng coin. Baddeley asked Els if he needed the marker moved, but Els said no. Moments later, Els's ball hit the marker and was misdirected away from the cup. "I had to laugh at myself because it was just a total amateur mistake," Els recalled. "I should have had him move it. I mean, he was marking it with a freakin' English pound." Holding his thumb and finger about an inch apart, Els said, "The thing is about this high."

Unlike many of their earlier counterparts, today's pros are as apt to hit the shrink's couch as they are the driving range.

The noted sports psychologist Bob Rotella estimates that 40 of the top 50 Tour pros work with sports psychologists. In fact, the 2001 British Open champion, David Duval, who's worked with Rotella since the golfer was in college, spends a weekend with Rotella prior to each season developing a game plan that he thinks lets him play his best competitive golf.

Said Rotella: "We talk about being in the greatest state of mind and mood every time you step onto a golf course, letting nothing faze you, getting into that bubble on the first tee that's close to being in a trancelike state."

The pros will tell you much of their golf success or failure depends on their swing coach, their sports psychologist, and other members of their entourage who help them keep focused.

Lee Westwood has a different theory. "So much depends on the previous night's film you watched in the hotel room." If pros watch a happy movie that lets them sleep through the night with good thoughts, they play well. But if they wind up watching something like *Hannibal*, they might get eaten alive on the golf course the next day.

Steve Flesch is one of the rare golfers on the Tour who think they know their own swing better than any "swing doctor" ever could. He has bucked the trend of Tour pros' having a posse of coaches, therapists, and gurus whispering in their ears.

Flesch says he knows his swing better than anyone else. "Having a coach would drive me nuts," said the player who earned nearly $1.2 million in 2002. "A coach can give you too much to think about. If I was good enough to get out here, I should be good enough to figure out what I need."

Tour player Brian Henninger, a self-taught late bloomer who had never worked with a golf coach, thought it was a good idea to have a coach analyze his swing. Wrong. "Oh, man, was that a mistake," he recalled. "I thought if I could understand my swing better, I could become a top-30 player. All I did was become a complete mess."

Many pros believe that no player ever faced a more pressure-packed putt than Bernhard Langer.

It was the last match, the last hole, and the last shot of the 1991 Ryder Cup at Kiawah Island, South Carolina. Langer stood over a six-footer. If he made it, the Europeans would retain the Cup. If he missed it, the Americans would regain the trophy. The six-time Ryder Cup member and two-time Masters champion struck his putt—and then watched in agony when it slid by the hole.

He later said it was one of the most stressful golf shots he ever attempted. The others? Each of the previous ones that put him in the position for that final putt. "It was every shot on the last four or five holes," he recalled. "I knew from the time I'd teed off on the 15th that the Cup would come down to my match."

Padraig Harrington credits his excellent putting ability to a strict routine he does for each and every putt outside of tap-in range.

Harrington, who finished second on the 2002 European Tour money list, looks at the ball from the east, west, south, and north. His all-encompassing read gives him four views of the contour. The lesson here is: you want to putt like Padraig, but you'd never want to play in the group behind him. His routine makes him one of the slowest golfers on Tour.

Rich Beem's wallet contains credit cards, cash, pictures of loved ones, and something you won't find in the wallet belonging to any other PGA Tour player—an ID card from his days as a Seattle salesman.

Beem, the winner of the 2002 PGA Championship, says the card is there to constantly remind him that no matter how bad things get on the Tour, he's still light-years ahead of where he came from. "I'm going to keep that card forever, just as a reminder it could always get worse," said Beem, who finished seventh on the 2002 money list, pocketing $2.9 million.

Beem's ability earned him the answer to a trivia question that will one day win a bunch of bar wagers: Who won his first major in which Tiger finished as the runner-up?

If Fred Couples appeared to look deep in thought while he waited to play the final hole of the 1992 Masters, it's because he was. Many historical thoughts are bound to ricochet through the head of a golfer as he stands on the threshold of greatness. It was no different with Couples.

Well, maybe a little different.

The tournament was effectively over, and Couples would win, but he had one thing on his mind before sinking the putt for the title. He turned to his caddie and said, "Can you believe the Knicks only scored thirty-seven points in the first half last night?"

He may have made it seem like a friendly, carefree ceremony, but Byron Nelson admitted to being a bundle of nerves each year on the first tee at Augusta National.

In fact, it was the only shot he practiced all year long. "It's the most difficult thing I do," Nelson admitted before turning 90 in 2002. "I practice more for that one thing than what I do the whole rest of the year. I worry about it for a month. That one shot detracts from everything else all week. It's been bothering me for quite some time."

Many of the honorary golfers confess to being a bundle of nerves during the ceremony and are simply hopeful they don't strike a spectator, as Sam Snead did in 2002.

Head Games

Not ever getting a hole in one does bother some pros.

In fact, it bothered the European Tour star Jamie Spence so much that he began seeing a hypnotherapist in 2002 in the hopes the tick-tock doc could unlock some door in Spence's mind that kept him from getting an ace.

The golfer was told to "visualize the ball going into the hole." Three tournaments after his session, Spence knocked home his first ace. Incredibly, he got his second the week after that.

Jesper Parnevik had a short par putt at the 1999 Loch Lomond Invitational in Scotland when he backed away, apparently deep in thought. He yanked the putt and bogeyed the hole.

When asked later what had thrown off his concentration, he said he and his caddie had a bet on who could solve a brainteaser math question about how long a rope would need to be to encircle the Earth three feet above the equator. Parnevik won the bet, but lost the tournament.

John Maginnes says that most professional golfers are so zeroed in on concentrating on their shot they don't realize they're playing in front of loud, often boisterous crowds.

He said he's always surprised by the loud cheers and applause that follow a clutch shot or putt. "When that happens, most of the time my first reaction is still, 'Where did all these people come from?'" Maginnes said. "Most of the time I have no idea people are out there watching us play golf."

Head Games

Pro golfers are notorious for having superstitions. For example:

Charles Howell III always tees up the ball in such a way that the club head will smack the ball's brand name.

Justin Leonard will always mark with the same coin—until he misses an easy putt.

Michael Clark II tries to wear underwear with holes in them.

Mike Weir? Well, he says he puts his putter in the toilet overnight to wash away the "evil lip-out curse." As for caddies, they avoid Weir the morning after a bad day of putting.

Self-taught Hale Irwin, the most successful player in the history of the Champions Tour, stays in shape by staying away from the golf course.

He deliberately avoids the game for long stretches because he believes it keeps him fresh when it's time to compete. "I try to get away from the game so when I come back I'll be back with renewed vigor. I think it would ruin my game to practice with a teacher, and I haven't watched an hour's worth of film in my life."

Ten days before he has to play, he begins hitting balls at the range. "I play myself into shape because the only way to get your game in shape is through competition."

When putting goes south, pro golfers have their own special sorts of nightmares.

Head Games

After Chris DiMarco's first year on the Tour in 1990, he was putting so badly that he lost his card. Throughout the following year, he would wake up in the middle of the night dreaming of game shows. "I used to have this nightmare where I'd be on *The Price Is Right*," DiMarco recalled. "They would have that little golf game, you know? I'd have this little two-footer and I'd miss it."

Fortunately, DiMarco doesn't get those nightmares anymore—he was eleventh on the 2002 money list with $2.6 million. And he putts much better.

Don't be fooled by that look of intense concentration when Ted Tryba's bending over a money putt on the 18th green. He's not thinking about the situation, the pressure, and the crowd. He's thinking about being home putting on the carpet on his living-room floor. "Focus on the putt, not the situation," he said. "If you get preoccupied with the situation, you'll probably screw up the putt."

Tryba knew he wanted to be a professional golfer at the age of seven, even thought he had lost all the vision in his left eye three years earlier when a stick punctured it, rendering him blind in that eye. Even with the disability, for Tryba there was no looking back.

Par for the Course

THE NAME TOM WATSON will long be remembered in the annals of British Open history. He won the championship five times, in 1975, 1977, 1980, 1982, and 1983. When asked to pick a favorite year, he said that it is sort of like having to choose between your children, but he did express being partial to three of them.

His top three: 1977, "when Jack Nicklaus and I sort of had a two-man tournament"; 1980, when Watson putted better than he ever had before or has since; and 1983, when "I never hit a better two-iron in my life than I did on that last hole"—to beat Andy Bean and Hale Irwin by a stroke.

Propriety forbids the ladies from ever seeing one of Payne Stewart's rarest autographs.

It's on a wall at the Pine Crest Inn in Pinehurst, North Carolina. He signed it the Monday before he won the 1999 U.S. Open at Pinehurst No. 2. A protective piece of Plexiglas was installed over the autograph after he won.

So why can't women see it? Stewart signed his moniker on the wall of the men's room.

The Ambush at Lajitas Golf Course in tiny, desolate Lajitas, Texas, has a lot of notoriety and history.

It's the place where General John "Blackjack" Pershing commanded a U.S. Cavalry Post when Pancho Villa and his revolutionaries threatened settlers in far West Texas. Comanches camped out here, staging raids into Mexico along the Rio Grande for horses and silver. The land also became part of the pony path named the Great Comanche War Trail.

But what makes this course so unique is it has an extra hole that is an international novelty. It features a tee in the United States and a green 100 yards away, across the Rio Grande River in Mexico. Unfortunately, you don't get your ball back. The lack of a proper border crossing within 100 miles makes it impossible to putt out without turning your round into an all-day affair. But golfers are welcome to try to ace it, although it won't count on the scorecard.

Jack Nicklaus tried to talk him out of it, but David Murdock, the man who made billions from Dole pineapple and had hired the Golden Bear to design Sherwood Country Club, insisted on it.

What is it? That danged large rock in the middle of the 16th fairway of the Thousand Oaks, California, course. Murdock was a huge *Little House on the Prairie* fan, and the rock marks the exact location of the house when the popular TV show was filmed there from 1974 to 1983.

Hell's Half Acre, one of golf's most famous sand traps at the 7th hole at Pine Valley Golf Club in New Jersey, is actually 1.2 acres of sand and brush.

Like the rest of Pine Valley, it has no rakes. Designer George Crump wanted it that way. He thought raked traps would not make the course punishing enough. There are federal prisons less punishing than Pine Valley.

It was the first course that Crump ever designed. Dressed in his favorite outfit of knickers, high-laced shoes, and floppy hat, Crump worked out his holes by hitting golf shots rather than by drawing sketches.

Construction began in 1913 with the removal of over 22,000 stumps, which had to be pulled out with special steam winches and horse-drawn cables because dynamite only blew up the sand around the stump. Marshlands were drained, dams built, and underbrush cleared away.

Believe it or not, throughout the 1960s a PGA Tour tournament was held at the Speedway at Indianapolis during the same week as the Indianapolis 500.

The golf course included 27 holes, a nine-hole course in the infield of the track, and a full 18-hole course outside the track.

The noted course designer Pete Dye had mixed emotions when the Tour came to his native Indiana to play the Brickyard course in 1960 in the 500 Festival Open. He was understandably proud, but also a little embarrassed. "That final round was played through an unholy mess of chicken bones, beer cans, programs, and wrappers," he recalled.

"The total purse was $50,000, which was a lot of money back then. As general chairman of the tournament, I remember sort of apologizing to [player] Mike Souchack for the ruckus and bad playing conditions. His response was, 'If you want to cut holes in the pavement, we'll play straight down Main Street for that kind of money.'"

Times, not to mention pampered Tour players, sure have changed.

Jack Nicklaus has been a leading advocate of keeping the specifications of golf balls within mortal standards. Like many purists, he believes the technology that enables golf balls to go farther will make some of the most storied courses—and records—in golf obsolete.

He was opposed to lengthening Augusta National Golf Club's fairways to suit the new balls' capabilities and sarcastically remarked, "Pretty soon, we'll be teeing off downtown somewhere."

The comment was duly noted by Augusta Chairman Hootie Johnson, and today a plaque at the 18th tee says simply, "Downtown."

Among the more interesting rules at Willie Nelson's Pedernales Golf Club in Austin is that no more than

12 people are allowed in each foursome and that there is no such thing as a lost ball because sooner or later someone is going to find it.

Short fences and long balls combined to cost the Laguna National Golf and Country Club, site of the 2003 Caltex Singapore Masters, a fortune in lost golf balls.

The range at the course is just 220 yards long. A fence was built to contain any longer shots, but the fence wasn't high enough and players routinely blasted the course's practice balls into the adjoining canal at the back of the range. A local newspaper reported that 400 dozen Titleist Pro V1s were lost in the drink and that the course had to resort to conventional low-compression range balls in order to keep shots from getting away.

Par for the Course

The first round of the 2002 Australian Open was canceled for unusual meteorological reasons. It wasn't snow, it wasn't rain, and it wasn't golf-ball sized hail. No, the reason was sunshine—days and days of endless sunshine.

The nonstop beautiful weather turned the greens at Victoria Golf Club so rock-hard that they were deemed unplayable for the first round. Well-struck balls would confoundingly ricochet off into distant hazards, and three-foot putts were rolling clear off the green. Still, the decision baffled many of the pros.

"I've never heard of an event canceled because of perfect weather," Rich Beem said.

Play resumed after greenskeepers softened the greens, but the tournament was cut to 54 holes. The Australian Steve Allan was crowned champion.

Amazing but True Golf Facts

PGA Tour Commissioner Tim Finchem's office overlooks the TPC at Sawgrass, and it's his home course. When asked for advice on how to best play the notorious 17th hole—an island green—Finchem says the solution is to think happy thoughts.

"I tell people the key to playing that hole is the power of positive thinking," he says. "I say, 'Don't let yourself think about how in one year ninety-eight of the world's best players knocked a ball into the water there.' That always drives 'em crazy."

The commish, a 4.8 handicapper, once hit a ball into the water there and followed the shot up by hitting the next one right into the cup for a par 3.

Many were wondering what exactly Augusta National would do next to prevent Tiger Woods from winning another Masters after he'd won his third in 2002 on a course that had been rebuilt specifically to make it more difficult for Woods to earn another green jacket.

Before his third Masters title, the holes were lengthened, trees were added, and one of the toughest golf courses in the world was made even tougher. Still, Tiger won.

His victory prompted *The Tonight Show* host Jay Leno to tell the following joke: "And you know they tried to make it harder for him to win this year . . . but it didn't work. So next year, do you know what they're doing? Every time he birdies a hole, he has to take a shot of tequila."

From 1860 to 1870, the first-place winner at the first British Open Championship was given a prize that had nothing to do with cups, trophies, or jugs.

No, the practical Scots from Prestwick, which held the tourney during those years, gave the winner the Challenge Belt, a red belt made of Moroccan leather, which members of the club paid for themselves.

Young Tom Morris was the last golfer to win the belt, in 1870. In 1872 (there was no championship in 1871) members had to pass the hat to pay for the fabled Claret Jug, which is to this day the cherished prize. Young Tom was the first winner of that one.

And what became of the Challenge Belt? Young Tom kept it and when he died, it remained in his family's possession.

Vijay Singh is considered one of the most dedicated practice men in all of golf. Where does he like to practice? The TPC at Sawgrass in Ponte Vedra Beach, Florida.

Par for the Course

"There's a great putting green and a short-game area and tees that let you hit into different winds," he explained. "Plus the people in Ponte Vedra are used to seeing pros, so you don't get bothered like you do at Tour events."

Not coincidentally, Singh usually does well at the TPC during the Tour's spring stop there.

Arguably, the most politically incorrect golf course in the world is the Bagan Nyaung Oo Golf Club in the Southeast Asian country of Myanmar.

Golf-loving generals decided to build the course on a holy site and ignored pleas to protect the Bagan pagodas. The club is run strictly by the military.

On the plus side, the greens fee for 18 holes is only $30. Girl caddies cost an extra three dollars per round.

Champions Tour member Stewart Ginn lives in Malaysia and is one of golf's most well traveled men. He's won 16 different tournaments all over the world.

While most of his colleagues are used to seeing finely manicured greens, Ginn remembers being astounded at how they tend to the greens at the oldest course outside Britain, the Royal Calcutta Golf Club in Calcutta, India. "A guy cutting the greens for the championship in 1995 was pushing with a hand mower and another guy was pulling it," he said. "No ride-on mowers, no power mowers. One was pushing and one was pulling as they cut the greens on a course for a major championship. I thought that was so unique to see on a golf course."

Frank Nobilo had a devil of time at the 1994 U.S. Open at Oakmont in the famed "church pews."

The distinctive bunker sits between and menaces both the 3rd and 4th holes and has eight rows of grass between the 30 yards of sand trap. Nobilo had a double bogey after visiting the bunker while playing the par-4 3rd hole during the final round. It so unnerved him that he blames the bunkers for helping derail what had been a promising run at winning his first major.

"I had been leading the U.S. Open on the final day, and that double bogey rattled me," he recalled. "I bogeyed the next three holes and I was finished. The church pews did me in. Oakmont has the only church pews in the world where you go to cuss. Prayer won't help."

Men find it hard to par the second hole at the Golf de Andratx course in Mallorca, Spain.

The 161-meter par-3 hole is quite small, but it has a serious distraction. It sits next to a house owned by the German beauty Claudia Schiffer. However, getting a peek at Claudia isn't easy because the house is "paparazzi-proofed," with towering walls and hedges obscuring the view to prying lenses and eyes.

But the possibility of seeing her is exciting, and you will always be reminded of her presence because on the scorecard the hole is labeled "Casa Claudia." Claudia herself plays golf once in a while.

When Greg Norman began building the second course for Lansdowne Resort near Leesburg, Virginia, in 2002, he decided he needed to make it, gulp, 7,400 yards long. He said he was taking into account that professionals in the 1980s could drive the ball 265 to 275 yards. Now that distance is up to 310 to 320 yards.

Also, he decided to make the last four holes cover exactly 1,760 yards: one mile. According to Norman, "That's so if there is an event here, the announcer will have the opportunity to say, 'Now they're getting down to the hardest mile in golf.'"

You wouldn't think the small state of Massachusetts would even have room for it, but the Bay State is home to the world's longest golf course. It's the International Golf Club in Bolton, an 8,325-yard monster that includes a 715-yard par-6 5th hole and one of the world's biggest greens (33,840 square feet).

Since 1983, more than a hundred courses have been built in Communist China.

In Shanghai alone you will find 15 courses. Before the arrival of the Communists, there was only one course. Most of the caddies in Shanghai are Japanese. They will shout "Nice on!" if you hit the green—a Japanese adaptation of an English phrase. The pitching wedge is called a *pitchi*.

The actor Will Smith may be famous for being one of the *Men in Black*, but he'd rather be a man on the green.

Par for the Course

He's such an avid golfer, he laid out $250,000 to join the exclusive Sherwood Country Club in Ventura County, California. Not only that, he then built a par-3 hole in his backyard with two different tees so he can hit balls from 105 to 150 yards out.

In between films, Smith often spends hours at home on the range working on his short game.

Bobby Jones and Alister MacKenzie codesigned Augusta National, but that doesn't mean Jones enjoyed any kind of advantage at the fabled course. Believe it or not, he never broke par in the Masters in the 12 times he played it, between 1934 and 1948.

He did, however, fire an impressive 64, but that was during a practice round.

Joe King, a Pennsylvania tree carver, did his best to give the much-traveled legend Arnold Palmer some real roots.

Palmer commissioned King to carve two identical statues of himself executing his free-swinging follow-through. The statues, which stand 14 feet high and are carved from trees, are located at two Palmer courses: The Signature at West Neck in Virginia Beach, Virginia, and the Arnold Palmer Signature Course at Stonewall Resort near Weston, West Virginia. The courses opened within months of each other in 2002.

Palmer hired King after admiring the job he had done to turn a once stately royal pine into an homage of Arnie's father, Deacon Palmer, at Latrobe (Pennsylvania) Country Club. The tree had been planted by Arnold and his dad when Arnie was a lad. The statue is of Deacon Palmer looking over the country club where his son has his roots.

Par for the Course

It took a team of 80 tree surgeons three days to dig up a 65-foot tree and move it less than 2,000 yards.

Why all the fuss? The tree was replacing the big dead pine that once fronted the fabled 18th green at Pebble Beach Golf Club. When the old one died, it didn't seem right to just plop a seedling there and pray for rain. After all, the old tree had been seen by millions each year and played a role in some of the most memorable shots in all of golf.

For the replacement tree, experts selected a disease-resistant cypress near Pebble's opening hole and had the 80-man gang dig up the tree, roots and all. Then it was moved along a winding path until it made it to its new ocean-view home on the 18th. Great pains were taken to make sure the tree was properly oriented in relation to the sun, so it faced the same way it had before its move.

The cost? $350,000.

On Phil Mickelson's first course-design effort, the magnificent
Whisper Rock Golf Club in Scottsdale, Arizona, for which he
collaborated with Gary Stephenson, Mickelson decided to
have a little devilish fun at golfers' expense.

Several of the holes feature optical-illusion sand traps
that peek up above what appears to be the green but in fact
are nearly 20 yards from the putting surface. Then there is
the par-5 third hole, which has a three-foot vertical-drop rock
"ha-ha wall." The name comes from eighteenth-century multi-
level English gardens and the reaction gardeners had when
someone walking on a top level fell off a wall because they
didn't know there was a drop.

The Old Course at St. Andrews originally had only 11 holes.
Golfers played the 11 holes out to an estuary and then turned

around and played the same ones back in again for a round of 22. The outward-bound players had to give way on the greens to the inward-bound golfers.

In 1764, members of the club decided the first four holes were too short so they converted them to two, and that is how today's standard 18-hole round of golf was created.

More ground was acquired in 1870, allowing for the creation of the now-famous double greens, which helped ease congestion. With more and more golfers playing, the course was played clockwise one week and counterclockwise, as it is played now, the following week. This gave the course the respite it needed from "excessive wear and tear," with hardly any maintenance involved.

At least once a year, officials at St. Andrews let golfers play the course clockwise, the way it was played for most of the nineteenth century.

Ben Crenshaw uses a decidedly low-tech way to design championship greens—he studies potato chips.

During the early design stages of Kapalua Golf Club's Plantation Course on Maui in Hawaii, Crenshaw was eating a bag of potato chips with the developers of the seaside resort when one of them asked what kind of computer program he planned to use to design the undulations of the greens. Crenshaw said he wouldn't dream of entrusting such calculations to a computer. Instead, he pulled out a chip from a bag he was snacking on and said, "This is the 18th green."

He proceeded to lay out the course using chips that had the undulations he wanted. The chips were later used as models for the actual greens he and Bill Coore designed.

During the 2002 Michelob Championship, the high rough at the Kingsmill Golf Club made some golfers' hair stand on end.

It was a particularly rough rough for golfers who consider themselves vertically challenged.

Hedemichi Tanaka, a 5-foot-6 Tour player, said the rough was so high it covered his ankles and made him think about changing some equipment most golfers wouldn't consider changing. When asked how he combats the rough, Tanaka said: "For a player of my height, it is very difficult. I have to start wearing higher shoes."

Arguably, the club with the best players in golf is the Champions in Houston, a course cofounded by Jimmy Demaret and Jackie Burke, two Tour legends renowned for being serious about the game they love.

The club is home to more single-digit handicappers than any other local club in golf. It has 400 members, all of whom must play to a 15 or better handicap just to apply.

And membership in the club doesn't give the golfer the right to any lessons from Burke, a man who's scornful of golf gurus, even though many of them learned from him. "If they can't beat you," Burke says, "they've got nothing to teach you."

The most famous voice in British Open golf doesn't belong to a player or broadcaster. In fact, the voice belongs to a man most golfers have never even heard of: Ivor Robson.

Since 1974, Robson has introduced the players to the gallery at the British Open as they tee off on the first tee. Twice every 11 minutes, he calls out each player's name for the worldwide audience. He's on the job from 7 A.M. to 4 P.M., without even the most personal of breaks being allowed.

Par for the Course

Jeweler Alec Harvey has been carving the names of British Open champions on the Claret Jug since 1967. He'd like to see a fellow Scot win, especially if it's his son, Colin Montgomerie. That would please him, although, he admits, "That's a lot of letters."

Harvey doesn't start carving early, no matter how sure a thing the outcome seems. For instance, he declined to begin engraving the name of Jean Van de Velde in 1999, even though the Frenchman seemed a shoo-in to win. Van de Velde needed a double-bogey 6 on the final hole of the Championship to win, but wound up taking a 7, sending the match into a four-hole playoff that eventually was won by Paul Lawrie.

Many golfers disparage a course they don't like by calling it a "goat track." They might think differently if ever given the chance to tee it up at Lahinch, often called "The St. Andrews of Ireland."

The course, created in 1893 by Old Tom Morris, is home to a herd of goats that graze the fairways and proudly adorn the club's logo. The goats serve as natural barometers and have a sixth sense as to when bad weather is approaching. When the goats are on the clubhouse porch, golfers know they have a few minutes to get inside before the weather turns nasty.

Par for the Course

Many people dream of finding the time and the $350 needed to play Pebble Beach. That might seem like a lot of money to play golf, but then again, it is Pebble Beach.

So how much dough do you need to live there? Try $29.5 million. That's how much a 6,500-square-foot house behind the 13th green was listed for when it went up for sale in 2003. The six-bedroom, nine-bath home was one of the locations for the 1944 Elizabeth Taylor movie *National Velvet*.

A New Jersey company is specializing in keeping pesky geese off greens, where they ruin the putting surface with their uncivilized behaviors. The secret: border collies. The restless animals love running and are tireless in chasing geese away. The company is called Geese Police Inc. and sells trained border collies to golf courses.

Right on the Money

WHEN IT COMES TO WACKY ODDS on wacky bets, the place to go is always Ladbrokes. It's the group that gives 1-to-4 odds each year that someone will streak at the British Open Championships.

They're also the ones who still say Tiger Woods is a 500-to-1 shot to someday become president of the United States.

Woods, while expressing no interest in ever running for office, responded by saying if he did run for president, he'd probably use the same campaign slogan that helped him win election as his class president in high school: "Longer lunches and less homework!"

Right on the Money

A popular practice round betting game on Tour is called "thousand-dollar-no-bogeys." The pros each commit to paying anyone in their respective foursome $1,000 if they make it through the practice round without a single bogey.

It's particularly tough at major venues like Scotland's Turnberry, where in 1994, Corey Pavin, Ben Crenshaw, Davis Love III, and Brad Faxon agreed to a game. Crenshaw was out on the second hole; Love on the 12th, and Pavin a couple of holes later. That left Faxon against three guys with a vested interest in seeing him blow up.

Faxon, in an interview with *Golf Digest*, said that what ensued was one of the greatest times he's ever had on a golf course. "During those last four holes, the three of them were rooting against me out loud right to the point of contact. As soon as I hit my ball on 18, I offered them each a buyout for $975. Nobody took it. I made my par and they all paid me

$1,000. It took awhile, but I got a check from every one of them. Somebody's wife wasn't too happy, though."

Phil Mickelson bet Mike Weir that Jim Furyk would hole a sand shot to prolong an outstanding sudden-death duel with Tiger Woods at the 2001 NEC Invitational at Firestone.

Weir agreed to give Mickelson 25-to-1 odds for the $20 bet. Easy money? Not for Weir. Furyk holed it. No word on whether Furyk got a cut of Mickelson's $500 winning wager.

When officials of the PGA Tour found out about the bet, they said it was a "technical violation" of the Tour's anti-gambling policy. Mickelson and Weir were not fined, but they did have to submit to a lecture from PGA Tour commissioner Tim Finchem.

Right on the Money

According to a survey reported in *Golf* magazine, 78 percent of amateur golfers said they would pay an instructor $1,000 if he could guarantee them he could make them a scratch golfer within one year. One percent were so desperate, they claimed that they would shell out up to $100,000 if those magic results could be ensured.

Interestingly, $1,000 is the amount the famed teaching pro Butch Harmon charges for just one hour of instruction.

The survey results also indicated that for 2 percent of golfers, improving their course management was the most important goal, while 1 percent want to improve trouble play. Those are the two areas where most instructors say golfers need the most help.

Amazing but True Golf Facts

The top 125 golfers in 2002—those who retain Tour privileges—earned at least $500,000 that season, and 61 of them earned over $1 million.

More typical are the strugglers like Jeff Brehaut, who earned $274,335 in 2002 and finished 161st in earnings. He figures it costs him about $100,000 a year to cover expenses at the 26 to 27 tournaments he plays each year. And, no, most of those expenses don't involve lobster lunches at the Ritz-Carlton.

"You have guys going first class, but there are a lot of guys like me going in coach," said Berhaut.

One hundred and ninety-eight golfers earned at least $100,000 on the Tour.

He played in only six PGA Tour events in 2002 and missed the cut in five of them. And in the one tournament in which he did make the cut, the 2002 Tampa Bay Classic, he earned a measly $8,620.44 for finishing in a tie for forty-first. But Ty Tryon was still a corporate darling. That's because in 2001, at the age of 17, he became the youngest golfer ever to earn a Tour card.

His agent, Jay Danzi of IMG, says, "Companies view Ty as someone who's going to have a great career for years to come. Ty needs to feel comfortable and believe in the products. We've turned down lots of opportunities."

Still, the swinging teen earned well over $1 million endorsing Callaway and Target products.

Few people would guess that the top taxpayer in all of Shenzhen, China, in 2001 was none other than Tiger Woods.

The world's number one golfer paid 4.2 million yuan ($500,000) in taxes on his undisclosed appearance fee during a promotional tournament at the prosperous financial center near Hong Kong. The area is home to a number of well-to-do Chinese.

The news that Woods paid more in taxes than anyone else in the People's Republic of China—a country of 1.3 billion— made headlines around the world. When told of this dubious distinction, Woods said, "That's actually pretty funny. . . . But it's not that funny."

Course designer Tom Fazio gets much of the blame for today's golf being so expensive, but then again he points out that we're not going to see a $2,500 Chevy again.

Still, when his uncle George Fazio started back in the 1960s, it cost $10,000 to build a hole. These days, it often costs Tom Fazio $200,000 to $400,000 to build one hole, and some of his courses, like Shadow Creek Golf Club in Las Vegas, cost $37 million to build.

Rookie Mike Nicolette got a heady introduction to life on the PGA Tour when he found himself paired with Seve Ballesteros and Greg Norman at the final round of the 1983 Bay Hill Classic.

Nicolette, who was struggling just to pay his bills, overheard Seve talk about his extensive holdings in Spain, and Norman talk about the $75,000 Ferrari he'd just purchased. "At the time, I'd been worrying about my next rent payment," recalled Nicolette.

He certainly must have been hungry, because he beat Norman in a playoff for his first Tour victory.

Arnold Palmer remembers the motivation for succeeding at golf back in 1954 when he was a Tour rookie and the total prize money for the entire season was $750,000.

He said he knew that if he didn't become one of the top two players on the Tour, he would have to return home and work in a Pennsylvania coal mine.

Today, players from all over the world come to the United States to compete for nearly $250 million in PGA Tour prize money.

Rich Beem was such a long shot to win the 2002 PGA Championship that oddsmakers didn't even have him listed when the odds of potential winners came out. After he did win by holding off a charging Tiger Woods, *USA Today* asked odds-maker Danny Sheridan to calculate what the odds would have been for picking Beem as the winner. Sheridan said they were 250,000 to 1.

Tour pros should pick their sponsors wisely. Sponsors not only pay their pros big bucks, but they're also happy to help their coddled players in times of need.

When a freak ice storm knocked over some towering trees in the yard of Tour player Matt Gogel's Kansas home in 2002, he called his sponsor, Davey Trees, to come clean up the mess. "We had four trucks and an army of guys out here cleaning up," he recalled. "The neighbors couldn't believe it."

Chances are decreasing that you'll ever get to chat with a professional golfer on a commercial flight—not even if you fly first class.

Amazing but True Golf Facts

More and more of the pros are opting to fly the friendly skies on a private jet. At the 2001 Marconi Pennsylvania Classic, Rocco Mediate revealed how "affordable" private jets have become. He worked out a deal where he bought 50 hours of flying time per year for $206,000. Mediate earned his yearly airfare—and then some—that week by finishing second, to earn $290,400.

Talk about trickle-down economics. After Retief Goosen won the 2001 U.S. Open and pocketed a cool $1 million, you'd expect to see his wife, family, and friends enjoying some of the spoils. But his sports psychologist? Goosen's Belgian mind doctor, Jos Vanstiphout, was seen flashing around town in a brand-new Ferrari—a gift from Goosen.

Right on the Money

PGA pro Chris DiMarco remembers the days when he and his wife were living in a cramped apartment complex and had less than $1,000 in their savings account.

Then his golf game caught fire. In the year 2000 he posted 10 top-25 finishes and pocketed $576,000 for winning the SEI Pennsylvania Classic. He earned over $2.6 million in earnings in 2002. Now if he wants to buy something, he doesn't even look at the price tag. To him, the incredible money means there's "no sense of reality on Tour. Zero."

The 2002 New Zealand Open was considered a bust in many circles after Tiger Woods reportedly was given $2.5 million just to play in the tournament of the homeland of his caddie, Steve Williams. The fee was so exorbitant that many fans groused about the subsequent increase in ticket prices, and some competitors publicly considered backing out in protest.

Despite the fee, it wasn't an altogether winning weekend for Woods, either. He putted horribly and finished tied for a distant sixth behind the winner, Craig Perry, who joked, "I can't remember the last time I beat Tiger."

For beating Tiger and everyone else, Perry earned $76,000 or $2,424,000 less than Tiger got for poking his tee into the ground on the first hole.

Taking a cue from Woods, Perry asked for an appearance fee of $35,000 to travel there to defend his title in 2003. But Peter Dale, head of the New Zealand Golf Association, told him to forget about it. "We were willing to pay his airfares and accommodation and even toss in a fishing trip and get him out to the America's Cup. But we just can't pay appearance fees."

So Perry skipped the fishing and the sailboats to play instead at the 2003 Sony Open in Hawaii. "It's frustrating," he said at the time. "I wanted to go back and defend." But only for a price.

Tour scheduling conflicts put lucky Ernie Els in an awkward spot. As the defending champion at both the 2002 Ford Championship at Doral in Miami and the 2002 Dubai Desert Classic, Els was obligated to play at both in 2003. But the tournaments were scheduled for the same March weekend. Els opted for the desert venue, most likely because of the hefty appearance fees used to lure pros overseas. He finished second in the 2003 tourney.

A Tiger Woods rookie card from a 1996 *Sports Illustrated for Kids* magazine sold in 2001 for $125,000. That doesn't mean if your kid has the issue and you can locate the intact card that your kid's college education is in the bank.

At least 60,000 of the magazines were printed, all of them on a type of paper that is cheap compared to that used for store-bought trading cards. What happened was that in a moment of foolishness following Tiger's four straight major victories (three in 2000 and one in 2001), a fevered buyer thought the market would erupt and the card would become the Honus Wagner of golf cards.

"The $125,000 sale to an unidentified buyer has been verified," said Chris Ivey of the Dallas-based company Heritage Sportscards. "Others have since sold for $100,000, $51,000, and $22,000, but the first guy paid $125,000 because he thought his card would be the only PSA 10 [Professional

Sports Authenticator graded card on a scale of 1 to 10] in existence."

The original buyer soon found out he had paid too much. Today, the card is worth between $150 and $350.

Duffers and Hackers

THE DIXIE CHICKS, the popular female country group that sang the national anthem at the 2003 Super Bowl, apparently have some golfers in their henhouse.

According to the group's tour contracts, promoters must arrange for quality golf or the Chicks' feathers will get ruffled. The contracts stipulate: "Event coordinator must provide six tee-time passes with carts at a local par-72 championship-level course. Approx. tee time is 10 A.M. Please coordinate with Dixie Chicks Production Coordinator."

Duffers and Hackers

Former San Francisco 49ers quarterback Steve Young has faced down some mean hombres in his day, but one of the most stinging blows he was ever dealt was struck by a gentle 65-year-old known for wielding nothing meaner than a pencil.

Young was playing at Pebble Beach one year during the AT&T Pebble Beach National Pro-Am with Johnny Miller and Peanuts creator Charles Schulz, who was 65 at the time and still a pretty fair golfer. The trio was waiting for the fairway to clear at the 15th when, as a way of making small talk, Schulz blitzed the old QB from the blindside. Recalled Young, "He said, 'You're really bad. That must be embarrassing.' I thought nobody had really noticed. But that did give me the incentive to really improve."

The employees at the splendid World of Golf on Forty-seventh Street just up from the United Nations Building in New York

City are to be forgiven if they still mourn the death of the late King Hassan II of Morocco. The golf-mad royal may have been the biggest club junkie in the history of golf. He often spent more than $100,000 a year on the latest and greatest golf equipment, and paid extra to have the store reopen when he wanted to go on a shopping spree.

One time, the king learned that World of Golf had a new Ram Tom Watson lob wedge. He called them up and said he wanted it—no, *had* to have it. The store said it could have it to him in a swift two days. That wasn't good enough for the king, who sent a jet from Morocco to pick up the club and get it back to him the same day.

The lesson? It's good to be king.

Duffers and Hackers

Everyone knows that Fidel Castro was a fine ballplayer before deciding to pursue other pastimes, but did you know he was a golfer too?

During the 1959 Cuban Revolution, he and Lt. Che Guevara often played at the Colina Villa Real Golf Club. Guevara was a single handicapper and always won—until Castro ordered the course plowed under to make way for a military base. A Commie—and a sore loser.

Vini "Maddog" Lopez hasn't always been the caddie master at the Deal (New Jersey) Golf & Country Club. It just looks that way. His job is to open the course, get the players out, keep them happy, and oversee the club's 60-cart fleet. You'd think that would leave him plenty of time to wonder, "What if I had stayed at my other job."

The 53-year-old Lopez used to be the drummer for Bruce Springsteen and the E Street Band. In fact, he played, and receives credit, on the band's first two early 1970s albums, *Greetings from Asbury Park*, and *The Wild, the Innocent, and the E Street Shuffle.*" He left over a dispute with management.

"I used to wonder what would have happened if I'd stayed with the band. Now, I get up early and go to bed early. It's a normal life."

A 21 handicapper, Lopez says the song that most describes his game is "Darkness on the Edge of Town."

Of all the golfers who've ever spent time in the Oval Office, only one was known to have enjoyed a round of golf at fabled St. Andrews during his honeymoon.

Duffers and Hackers

It was Franklin Delano Roosevelt, who was an outstanding golfer renowned as one of the longest drivers in New York before polio put him in a wheelchair and destiny led him to become one of America's most revered presidents.

Ever wonder what a top hockey goaltender is thinking when the action is way down at the other end of the ice? If you're Stanley Cup champion John Van Biesbrouck, you might be thinking, "How could I three-putt from twelve feet on 17 today?" He admits his thoughts sometimes stray to golf when the play is down at the other end. "I'm not talking all the time, but there are times I am thinking about golf," he said. "It's an addictive game."

Amazing but True Golf Facts

Jerome Travers might have been the best golfer who couldn't care less. Though Bobby Jones, Tiger Woods, and Walter Travis are the only other men to win at least three U.S. Amateurs, Travers won four. He even won the 1915 U.S. Open, but cared so little he didn't even bother to show up to defend his title. At the ripe old age of 28, he quit the game for good.

President Woodrow Wilson may have been our nation's most golf-obsessed president.

He was known to play six rounds a week in all kinds of weather. In winter, he'd golf with red balls so he could see them in the snow. His caddie was required to carry a flashlight for night golf, and the president once played a match that did-n't end until 5 A.M. He considered the game a delightful pas-time and didn't care for its competitive elements so he never kept score.

"What did you say?" Those words sent a chill up the spine of 34-year-old Doug Mauch, director of golf at the Tradition Golf Club in La Quinta, California. They were uttered by Arnold Palmer, who had overheard Mauch pointing out flaws in Arnie's swing.

Mauch swallowed hard and gave Palmer, who was in a terrible slump, a complete rundown of what he needed to do to get his golf back on track. Palmer took the advice and shot a respectable 78 at the opening round of the 2002 Hope Desert Classic.

During the glory years of Frank Sinatra's Rat Pack, the actress Jeanne Carmen not only was Ol' Blue Eyes' lover and Marilyn Monroe's best friend, she also was famous as golf's sexiest trick-shot artist. One advertisement showed her standing looking out over a prone photographer with her ample assets pointing heavenward. The caption reads: "This is how Jeanne Carmen would look to the average golf ball."

Hollywood golf teacher Ron del Barrio was playing with Jack Nicholson when the pair came upon comedians Jon Lovitz, Dana Carvey, and the late Phil Hartman. Carvey started doing his impression of Nicholson. "Jack laughs and we're all having fun," del Barrio recalled. "We play through and Jack says, 'Nice guys . . . Who the hell were they?' I say 'Jack, that was Phil, Dana, and Jon from *Saturday Night Live*. Don't you every watch the show?' He says, 'I watch it every @#$*# week. Wouldn't miss it for the world.'"

You don't usually think of the name Frank Lloyd Wright when you talk about great golf architects, but the famous designer is the genius behind the fabulous clubhouse at the Grand Waikapu Country Club on Maui.

The blueprints originally were intended to be the basis for a Connecticut dream house for the playwright Arthur Miller and Marilyn Monroe, but their divorce ended that dream. Today, the building is considered one of the finest and most widely photographed clubhouses in all of golf.

It looks like he's having a great time, but Chevy Chase was anything but happy during the filming of the 1980 golf classic *Caddyshack*.

He claimed that most of the crew was inebriated, there was no script, and the set was often in chaos. Chase said he'd seen more professionalism in high school productions. The effect on Chase was so bad that he was repeatedly heard screaming to anyone who would listen, "I can't work like this!"

Amazing but True Golf Facts

It took actor Kevin Costner 86 takes to hit the shot in *Tin Cup* in which he banks a ball off a portable toilet and onto the green, rolling right up to the camera lens. In all, the scene took most of a day to shoot but lasted just 10 seconds on film.

Actor Kurt Russell literally got outfoxed during a golf outing at Snowmass Lodge and Club near Aspen in 2001.

Twice during one round, he hit drives down the fairway, only to see each ball snatched by a fox that scurried out from the rough. Apparently, the animal thought the balls were tasty eggs. But a local girl chased the fox and grabbed the balls after the fox dropped them. She returned with the balls and charged the actor $5 to get them back.

President Calvin Coolidge's 1925 inaugural address included the telling line, "Economy is idealism in its most practical form." The man was especially economical when it came to golf balls. An avid golfer, Silent Cal purposely hit only short shots so he wouldn't risk losing his ball.

It's a good thing the man died nearly 70 years before the introduction of the pricey Pro VI's. Of course, if you don't hit 'em far, you end up hitting 'em more often. Coolidge is not considered one of the finer golfers ever to play the game while being the occupant of the Oval Office.

Amazing but True Golf Facts

Dan Quayle's passion for golf has caused him to break one of the cardinal rules of politics—disagreeing on the record with the man who chose him to be his vice president.

Quayle thinks former President George H. W. Bush is wrong, wrong, wrong in his approach to golf. "I'm all for fast play, but he wants to get in a round in two and a half hours or less," says Quayle. "He just races through it. That's no way to play golf. It's like he has a list of all the things he wants to get done during the day and when he gets to 'Play golf' on the list, he wants to cross it out and move on to the next thing as fast as he can."

Hall of Famer Ted Williams used to say that hitting a baseball was the most difficult achievement in sports.

But did the Splendid Splinter ever try to slide a downhill 10-footer into the cup with two skins on the line? If he did, he might reevaluate his belief.

216

According to putting guru Dave Pelz, pros make about half of their putts from six feet out and less than 20 percent of their putts beyond 12 feet.

Some of the most promising future members of the PGA Tour spent an unnerving 10 minutes topping balls, digging divots, and making shots at the Q-school range that would embarrass beginners. What happened? They were trying to golf like Josh Broadaway.

The 25-year-old Albany, Georgia, golfer learned baseball before he learned golf: cross-handed. With the club pointed down, the right-hander grips it with his left hand below his right one. Not since Charley Owens played that way in the 1970s has a player made it cross-handed on Tour.

Amazing but True Golf Facts

Judd Swarzman is the king of the pro-ams. By 2003, the 65-year-old financial planner from Encino, California, had played in 27 pro-ams in 10 years and had spent more than $120,000 for the privilege. He's received more than 230 shirts, 25 pairs of shoes, 15 golf bags, and more than 50 dozen golf balls as tee prizes.

He says he would rather splurge on playing in tournaments than on fancy vacations, cars, or anything else. He was hooked on pro-ams after being paired with Gary Player at his first event. During the round, Swarzman told the golfer he was planning a South African vacation. Player invited him to stay at his home in South Africa. Player said Americans had been so nice to him over the years he was simply reciprocating. Swarzman accepted and the two have been friends ever since.

The Latvian hockey import Sandis Ozolinsh had to learn two languages when the hockey sensation joined the NHL in 1992: English and golf—because that's what his teammates spoke and talked about. Today, "Ozo" is such a committed golfer he spent $4 million to build Ozo Golf Club, the first golf course in his homeland, the Republic of Latvia.

During an exhibition match between two of baseball's greatest legends, Ty Cobb beat Babe Ruth 3-and-2 at Grosse Ile Golf and Country Club, near Detroit.

For Cobb, who had practiced tirelessly for weeks, the match meant so much to him that he put the cheap-looking winner's trophy right next to his Baseball Hall of Fame plaque on his mantel at home. On the other hand, Ruth, whose preparation consisted of just one practice round, viewed the match as nothing more than a friendly game. During the match he frequently drew laughs from the gallery by pretending to nap on the green while Cobb studied his putts.

After his legendary baseball career was over, Cobb had celebrity, time, and wealth. He put most of his energy into golf and was able to play free at most of the country's best courses and also got lessons in Georgia from home-state native Bobby Jones. Still, one of baseball's greatest hitters—who swatted fastballs, curveballs, and sliders better than anyone else—never mastered a confounding game where the ball stood absolutely still.

The exhibition victory over Ruth was Cobb's lone achievement in the game.

Fandemonium

EVEN THE MOST POPULAR GOLFERS hear from detractors who like to take potshots at the players.

Laura Davies got to say, "Take that!" to one such "fan" in 2002. He had written a scathing letter to the European Solheim Cup captain Dale Reid, complaining about her selection of Laura Davies over the Scottish golfers Janice Moodie and Catriona Matthew. The writer, who was so sure of himself that he signed his name and included his phone number in his rant, predicted Reid's team would lose and Davies would be the reason.

Reid passed the letter along to Davies, who called the man's phone number. She got the gentleman's answering machine, and left a tart message which concluded with a challenge to "put your money where your mouth is."

Although the Europeans lost, no one could pin the blame on Davies, who won two of her three matches. As for her detractor, he never called back.

Golf is a secondary event for many of the 30,000 people who attend the Phoenix Open. The biggest competition isn't on the course. It's trying to get a good spot at the Bird's Nest, a 44,000-square-foot hospitality tent located across the street from the TPC of Scottsdale.

"It's just a wild party," says Chip Tolleson, the advertising executive who oversees the operation; he begins planning in March for the next January party. The tent has 40 bars and is home to Duck Soup, a band that's been playing the tournament for 20 years. Each night more than eight thousand people crowd their way into the party pavilion. "It's the number one party at any golf tournament in the world," Tolleson boasts.

It's also one of the best places on the Tour for fans to get a chance to mingle with the pros.

Adulation follows Tiger Woods to the most unlikely places, as he found while winning the 2002 U.S. Open at Bethpage Black, on Long Island, New York.

After finishing the 14th hole, Woods was followed by a smiling throng when he dashed off to a nearby portable toilet. When he emerged from the stall, the crowd burst into applause. Woods looked puzzled and joked, "Are you guys clapping because I'm potty-trained? I made it this far, so don't you think I know how to go?"

Amazing but True Golf Facts

After each of his first 21 Tour victories, Phil Mickelson retrieved the flag from the 18th green and bestowed it upon Alfred Santos, 95, and his wife, Jennie. Mr. and Mrs. Santos put each flag up in the kitchen of their modest San Diego home.

In 2002, the Santoses politely asked Lefty to stop with the banners because there wasn't any more room. However, they said they would definitely make an exception if Mickelson were to bring them a flag from a major championship.

So who are Alfred and Jennie? They're Mickelson's maternal grandparents.

Pros like Tiger Woods don't like it when insincere autograph seekers try to make money off their names.

That's why observers were surprised when Woods signed an oil painting of Pebble Beach that a fan foisted on him during a practice round. Didn't he know that would be on e-Bay within the hour? "That's why I signed it in the lower right-hand corner. The frame will cover it up," Tiger explained.

You must have gone to Stanford, he was told. "Yeah," he responded, "I majored in sarcasm."

More than a few golf fans were whispering things like "Sissy!" when David Toms decided to lay up short of the water from a questionable lie in the short rough of the par-4 18th hole during the 2001 PGA championship. But Toms ignored his ego and the fans' slurs to make an up-and-down par for a one-stroke victory. Now, everyone calls him champion.

Toms said as soon as he sunk the putt that won the tournament, he could instantly tell that the crowd favored Phil Mickelson. "On the tape I can look past myself to the people in the crowd and only about one-third of them are cheering with me. I thought, 'Man, did I do something wrong or what?'"

Still, the man people thought was a fraidy cat had to laugh when they asked where he had gone to dinner the evening before his victory. "I'm almost embarrassed to say it—Chick-fil-A."

Nearly 1,000 spectators turned out to see 17-year-old Tour rookie Ty Tryon hit his first professional shot at the 2001 Phoenix Open.

But the front nine was far from historic for the youngest player ever to play on the PGA Tour. Tryon stumbled with a bogey-marred 43 that left fewer than 200 diehards tromping after him. Still, the high school junior was able to joke about it. "I scared them all off with my great performance."

For those who stayed, however, it will probably be an excuse to boast forever that they saw one of the game's greats play a round like a weekend hacker—that is, if Tryon lives up to his billing and actually becomes one of the game's greats.

The most famous streaker of all time is probably Mark Roberts.

According to the fanatically comprehensive website www.streaker.net, Roberts is the most prolific streaker ever, with more than 170 streaks under his, er, belt.

He dashed sans clothes across the 18th green at St. Andrews in 1995 while John Daly was celebrating his victory. On Roberts's back in thick black letters were the words "19th Hole" and an arrow that wasn't pointing to any nearby pubs.

When asked what he'd be taking with him after a rough week at the hands of Long Island hecklers during the 2002 U.S. Open at Bethpage Black, Sergio Garcia said, "A lot of new nicknames."

His constant waggle and gripping and re-gripping were too much for many outspoken golf fans, who shouted at Garcia whenever he wasn't moving quickly enough to suit them.

It also brought out some of the best from sports writers covering the event. Scott Ostler of the *San Francisco Chronicle* had this to say: "Golf according to John Daly: Grip it and rip it. Golf according to Sergio Garcia: Grip it and grip it and grip it and grip it and grip it and . . ."

Ben Crenshaw's Senior PGA Tour debut at the 2002 ACE Group Classic ended badly for him because he was distracted by some ardent fans of his. But he didn't mind. After all, the fans happened to be former President George H. W. Bush and his son, Florida Governor Jeb Bush, who arrived at the Naples, Florida, course with a large Secret Service detail.

Seeing his fellow Texans cheering him on seemed to rattle Crenshaw, who promptly bogeyed the 17th and quadruple bogeyed the 18th.

Afterward, he said he wasn't that upset with his poor finish. "I got to see the president and the governor," he said. "I don't care what I shot."

Tiger Woods is no stranger to difficult, pressure-packed situations on the golf course. But one he doesn't want to face again is being paired with the actor Joe Pesci and former NBA star Charles Barkley at a celebrity outing.

He said the noise level from the gallery was warlike and his playing partners' clubs were flying everywhere after flubbed shots, of which there were many. "It's safer to play two groups in front of them or two groups behind them," Woods said.

How rowdy and antagonistic U.S. fans were going to treat Colin Montgomerie at the 2002 U.S. Open became a concern to *Golf Digest*. The magazine printed up thousands of "Be Nice to Monty" buttons and distributed them to fans at Bethpage Black on Long Island, New York.

But Australian Steve Elkington had a more direct solution to people looking to upset Montgomerie, who has been known to suffer from a bad case of rabbit ears. "Colin needs to punch someone in the mouth," Elkington said. "Then the next guy who yells something will know he's got a good chance of getting his teeth knocked in."

The fans didn't have much chance to heckle Montgomerie. He had an early exit after missing the cut by one stroke.

Many grooms get into trouble golfing on their honeymoons. Not Stuart Meyers.

He met his future wife, Lee, at work and taught her to play. Three years later, he was still a 3 handicapper, but she was down to a 9.

The day of their wedding in 2002, Stuart and Lee played 18 holes at Pebble Beach in the morning. Instead of playing the 19th hole, the two immediately changed into wedding garb and got hitched right off the 18th green. The honeymoon involved lots of golf on the Monterey Peninsula, including rounds at Spyglass Hill and Spanish Bay.

British officials make only halfhearted attempts to stop streaking at the British Open. As Blackpool constable Jim Allen once explained: "You can't really prevent it, and it's not a serious problem. Everyone will have a good giggle and they'll hustle the streaker off the course."

Some are charged with a misdemeanor, but most first-time offenders at the tournament endure little more than a dressing down, if that's at all possible.

It wasn't anything like the dangerous missions conducted by the U.S. servicemen and -women, but Frank Lickliter, Mark Carnevale, Bill Kratzert, and Bob Dickson conducted some golf drills for military personnel at Guantanamo Bay Naval Base and Camp Delta in Cuba in 2002.

It all started when a Florida-based FBI agent, Mike Heard, was visiting and saw the decrepit conditions at the nine-hole course known as Yatera Seca, or "dry earth." Heard saw servicemen playing with 30-year-old clubs and rubber-coated miniature golf balls. "It's hard to explain how much my heart went out to them," Heard said. "Our people have given a lot for us. There are only a few things they can enjoy down there."

Golf is one of them.

Thanks to the PGA Tour–sponsored mission, the players delivered dozens of golf clubs and hundreds of balls for the golfers to enjoy when they take a break from defending freedom.

Still, there are some things even Tour pros can't change. When Lickliter asked what the course record was at Yatera Seca, he was told, "Eighteen holes without sunstroke."

Bag of Sticks

BEAUTY IS IN THE EYE OF THE BEHOLDER, but no one argues with ugly if it gets results.

In 2002, Phil Mickelson began using a back-weighted mallet-type putter with a horseshoe shape that he called "butt ugly." But for Mickelson, ugly works.

"I was hitting the ball too hard, trying to make it roll and hold its line," Mickelson says. "Now, I can hit it a little easier because the ball is rolling right off the face of the putter."

Mickelson and Titleist putter impresario Scotty Cameron worked together to make the ugly club so that Mickelson wouldn't keep missing those agonizing four-foot putts.

"The cosmetics of the putter are not important," he says. "It's the physics."

Smart pros know that once you find a club that works like magic, you should hold on to it.

Sam Snead used the same driver for more than 20 years.

Johnny Miller manufactured a little magic in his irons. In 1974 he acquired an old set of Tommy Armour 915T irons that "needed a little work." So Miller sawed down the long hosels and placed big gobs of lead directly behind the sweet spots. "Then I reground the top lines and soles until they were just right," he told *Golf Digest*. "Finally, I added True Temper Dynamic Shafts half an inch longer than standard in each club. The results were pure magic."

So pure, in fact, that Chi Chi Rodriguez, a very superstitious man, was convinced they were magic and pestered Miller to give them to him. Miller finally relented after Rodriguez did him a favor. But the clubs didn't work for Rodriguez the way they did for Miller. Rodriguez was convinced Miller had pulled a fast one on him and hadn't given him the "real" magic clubs.

Shingo Katayama, a crowd-favorite, is one of the only pros to carry five woods—a driver, a three, a four, a seven, and a nine—during tournament play.

On the practice range he carries another, a left-handed five-wood. He always starts out warming up left-handed, but he's not very good shooting from that side. He does it as a joke, explaining, "I love to hear the crowd say, 'How can he be a professional? He's not very good.' Then I turn around and start hitting right-handed."

Bag of Sticks

Champions Tour veteran Sammy Rachels probably put himself
in a hazardous situation when he called his three-iron, which
he no longer carries, his "mother-in-law club." When confused
reporters wondered what he meant, he said, "It's my mother-
in-law club because I want to hit it, but I can't."

Golfers are such rigid traditionalists that they will continue
to shun new equipment even if they know it can help them.
Take the belly putter, for instance.

Even the name provokes snorts of giggles. But the
resurrected putting proficiency of players who use the belly
putter—like Fred Couples, Vijay Singh, and Colin
Montgomerie—have turned ridicule into respect.

Montgomerie admits that many times he had to fight the
urge to leave his 47-inch belly putter in the locker when he

saw it poking up above his long irons in the bag. "I was acutely embarrassed when I first stepped out with the club," said Montgomerie. "I thought, 'How can things have come to this?'" But Montgomerie averaged one putt less per round in 2002 using the belly putter.

Vijay Singh, who played six years in Europe before finding fame in the United States as a PGA and Masters champion, was a notoriously poor putter who was constantly in search of the right club to help him master the greens.

From the time he was a teaching pro in Borneo to his success on the PGA Tour, it's estimated that Singh has used more than 60 different putters. In the past few years, he has worked incredibly hard on his putting, and Singh is now one of the best putters on Tour.

Bag of Sticks

The U.S. Open was not held during World War II. A worldwide shortage of rubber, a vital material to freedom-loving fighting forces, created a huge price spike in the availability and cost of golf balls. Many pro shops began charging exorbitant prices for balls and scavengers picked the woods and ponds clean as never before.

Others sought a different way to deal with keeping their golf-ball costs down. They played better. Then there were those who played prudently. For example, Sam Snead, a man with a reputation for frugality, played an entire four-day tournament with one golf ball.

When Johnny Farrell edged Bobby Jones in a playoff to win the 1928 U.S. Open championship, much fuss was made of the startling new technology he used to beat the great Jones and many wondered whether it would transform the game.

What was it? An aluminum-headed driver. Golf purists feared the newfangled club would ruin the game's grand traditions and called for a halt to any more deviations in club making. It was more than five decades before Eli Callaway introduced his Big Bertha.

Lee Trevino is one of the greatest pitchmen in the game. Fans love him for his wisecracking ways and his honest opinions. That's why Spalding relies on him to sell its products.

But during the Battle of Bighorn in 2002, Trevino thought it best not to play with, or tout, Spalding's new Top Flight balls. It wasn't that he didn't believe in the product. It's just that this wasn't the best time or place to show off the new ball because two of Trevino's playing partners, Sergio Garcia and Tiger Woods, were some big hitters. "I told Spalding, 'Sergio and Tiger will be outdriving me by a hundred yards,'" Trevino said.

Network golf announcers seem to know a golfer's exact yardage and the club he's using—even when their vantage point is far away. You'll hear them say something like, "And Tiger has 162 yards to the pin. He's using a knockdown seven-iron." So how do they know?

The golfer's caddie tells them. Tour caddies know Tour courses better than anyone, and networks wisely employ them to be spotters with headphones and mikes that link them right to an announcer's ear.

Slow play is a virtual impossibility in golf's fastest golf cart.

The Lamborghini EV2 Golf Cart is for the golfer who has everything except a sense of value. For $7,540, the cart can carry two bags, a cooler of beer, and more than 500 pounds of golfers at speeds of up to 15 mph.

For $1,100 more, the company will customize the engine so that your speed increases to 25 mph. Many of the golfers on the Champions Tour will make fun of any whippersnapper who buys one, recollecting when that much money could buy a real automobile.

Bag of Sticks

Tinkering with your own clubs can really pay off. It did for Dave Musty.

While still in the custom-home construction business, Musty, 49, decided to use scraps of maple wood to give his putter a sweet spot that Aunt Jemima would envy. His first time out, he one-putted the first eight greens and began thinking career change.

Today, his Musty Putters sell for up to $225 and are owned by golf-mad celebs such as Michael Jordan and Bill Murray.

The joke's so familiar that some golfers wonder whether it is true. Is the name "golf" an acronym for "Gentlemen Only Ladies Forbidden?"

Nah. It is believed the word golf originated with the medieval Dutch word *colf*, meaning "club."

Amazing but True Golf Facts

Golf's annual PGA Merchandise Show in Orlando always features top equipment and some outlandish new innovations in tees, trinkets, and accessories under the sprawling 1.1-million-square-foot roof of the Orange County Convention Center.

The extravaganza is a far cry from the very first national golf show, held in 1924 at the 71st Regiment Armory in New York City. The show was attended by Walter Hagen, Gene Sarazen, and the Australian trick-shot artist Joe Kirkwood.

But the biggest draw was the nine-hole, par-20 "Le Petit Golf" course. The glorified putt-putt course had water and bunkers and was 241 feet long; it was where the game's greats met to putt off against one another. Amazingly, the matches drew so much interest that *The New York Times* provided hole-by-hole coverage as if it were the U.S. Open.

Bag of Sticks

The rule that limits the number of clubs a golfer can carry to 14 came into being shortly after a conversation between two famed amateur golfers, Bobby Jones and Tony Torrance.

In the 1920s there was no limit to the number of golf clubs you could stuff into your bag. Because the clubs' shafts were made of hickory, they broke easily, and players used to carry copies of their favorite clubs. Walter Hagen used to have as many as 25 clubs in his bag.

When hickory became scarce and steel shafts were sanctioned, Jones and Torrance suggested having a rule that would limit the number of clubs. While discussing the ideal number, they looked into their own bags. Jones counted 16, Torrance 12. They split the difference and adopted a limit of 14.

Long-drive champion Jason Zuback uses many of the same tools as golfers everywhere when he blasts drives longer than

420 yards. But he uses one item most golfers aren't likely ever to use—at least not on the golf course. He swings so hard that the skin on his fingers tears and he has to use Krazy Glue to stick the skin back together.

He said his hands become like catcher's mitts from all the adhesive used to hold the skin on his fingers to his hands.

Toter Talk

TIGER WOODS SAID HE WOULD HAVE WON one less major if someone other than Steve Williams had been toting his bag during the dramatic playoff at the 2000 PGA Championship at Valhalla Golf Club in Louisville.

Before an approach shot in the playoff, Woods and Williams had conferred on the proper club and swing and Tiger settled in over the ball. Just then a gust of wind came up.

"The wind changed and Stevie called me off the shot, telling me to hit it harder than we'd planned," Tiger recalled. "He had the guts to do that." Tiger followed his caddie's advice and went on to beat Bob May in the playoff.

Amazing but True Golf Facts

Interrupting Tiger when he's standing over a ball is an indication of courage. Having Tiger listen to what you're saying is evidence of something else entirely: respect.

Jim "Bones" Mackay, Phil Mickelson's caddie, has to bite his tongue before 99.9 percent of Mickelson's imaginative, aggressive, and sometimes foolhardy shots.

The two have an agreement that Bones gets to veto one shot each year. He used it at the 2000 Compaq Classic when Mickelson, caught in high rough, wanted to skip a shot over water and onto the green. Mackay told him to hold off and try such water wizardry some other time—like when he was all alone playing a practice round with no one watching.

Toter Talk

Caddie Chuck Hoersch heeded nature's call rather than the rules and knocked his boss, the LPGA star Sophie Gustafson, out of the 2001 WPGA International Matchplay at Gleneagles.

Gustafson had won the last two holes to put her semifinal match against Laura Davies into a sudden death playoff. But before the playoff began, Hoersch went to the clubhouse bathroom. Hurrying back to the first tee, he accepted a ride in a marshall's golf cart.

Unfortunately, the rules state that players and caddies must walk at all times. The penalty was the loss of the hole in question. So Gustafson lost on the 19th hole before even taking a swing.

Jean Van de Velde's caddie, Christophe Angiollini, admitted he needed professional help after many blamed him for

Van de Velde's coming apart on the last hole during the 1999 British Open Championship at Carnoustie, Scotland.

The little-known Frenchman had a seemingly insurmountable three-stroke lead going into the 18th hole. A double-bogey 6 would have won it for him. Wielding a two-iron that Angiollini handed him to finish in style when he should have been laying up to protect the lead, Van de Velde hit the first of a series of disastrous shots on the 18th that led to a four-hole playoff. Scotland's Paul Lawrie, who started the day 10 strokes back, ended up winning in the greatest comeback in the history of major championships.

"I was hurting really badly for a long time," admitted Angiollini. "I had to take time off after what happened to me and it was 20 months before I could face carrying a golf bag."

Toter Talk

During a Nike Tour event in Mexico in 1995, David Toms was irked by his caddie when they reached the par-3 15th hole. The caddie kept telling him to use a six-iron and Toms kept saying, "No, it's a five-iron." The caddie persisted. The pro is usually going to win this kind of argument, and Toms did.

Using the stubborn caddie to increase his motivation, Toms teed off with his five-iron . . . and watched the ball land right in the cup for an ace.

When the round was over three holes later, Toms turned to the caddie and said, "You're fired."

Some caddies are such good golfers that they can beat the pros whose bags they tote.

On off days, caddies and their pros often go out for a friendly round. Usually there's a few bucks involved.

Amazing but True Golf Facts

One year, Mark Long, who loops for popular Fred Funk, won a nice bet from Funk after he beat his boss. Recalled Funk, "Yeah, it was a morning round on Valentine's Day. After he beat me and I'd paid him, he gave me ten bucks and said, 'Here, buy your wife some flowers for Valentine's Day and tell her they're from me.' Funny guy."

George Burns shot a blistering hot 7-under-par 65 during the 2000 AT&T Canada Senior Open and graciously deflected all the praise to his caddie, Stewart Bannatyne, who helped him read the greens at the St. Charles Country Club in Winnipeg, Manitoba.

It's not too unusual for a golfer to pay tribute to his bag toter, but in this case the 51-year-old pro was commending a caddie who was only 16 years old.

Burns was effusive in his praise following the round and gave all the credit to the youth, who had given him all the right reads. "The only putt I missed badly was on 16 and that's the only one I went against his read," Burns said. "It's the best I've putted in a long, long time, and I owe a lot to the youngster."

European Tour player Christopher Hanell's caddie has the unkind-sounding nickname "Two-Stroke Penalty." But it's really a compliment.

Hanell's caddie is Maria Nymoen, a beautiful blonde Swedish beautician. The word on the European Tour is that Maria's good looks are so distracting to Hanell's playing partners that they automatically shoot two strokes more than they normally would.

The highest paid athlete in New Zealand doesn't kick a ball, throw a pitch, or shoot at baskets. Nope, the highest-paid "athlete" in New Zealand carries Tiger Woods's bag. It's Steve Williams. He earns more than any other New Zealand–born sportsman, including top Kiwi rugby player, Jonah Lomu. In 2002, Tiger earned $7,392,188. Most PGA caddies earn between 5 and 10 percent of the player's total. That means Williams's take was between $365,500 and $730,000.

Not bad work if you can find it.

When not lugging the bag around, Williams likes to participate in a sport that allows him to go much faster than even a quick-paced round with Woods would allow. He's a race-car driver.

Toter Talk

Bruce Lietzke had more than just Tom Watson to worry about while defending his title at the 2002 SAS Championship at the Prestonwood Country Club in Cary, North Carolina. He was also up against the Philadelphia Eagles.

Lietzke, an avid Dallas Cowboys fan, was paired with Watson on the final round. But it was Watson's caddie, Bruce Edwards, who made life tough for Lietzke on the back nine when Edwards kept relaying the score of that day's Eagles-Cowboys game. It wasn't pretty for a Cowboys fan. Philadelphia won 44–13.

"I was pretty obnoxious to him [Edwards] when the Cowboys were good," Lietzke said. "I probably got what I deserved."

His Cowboys may have lost, but Lietzke didn't. He won the tourney with a 14-under 202 to beat Watson, who tied for second at 206.

Caddie Osman Juami thought his ship had come in when his employer, Zhang Lian Wei, birdied the final hole to win the 2003 Singapore Masters over Ernie Els.

But Zhang, who won $152,200, paid his caddie Juami just $700 for lugging his bag for seven straight days. Too bad for Juami his bag boss wasn't Vijah Singh. When Singh won the 2002 Singapore Masters, he paid his happy caddie, Poh Ah Chair, $24,000.

Holing Out

IN ITS PGA TOUR PLAYER SURVEY, *Sports Illustrated* revealed in 2002 that 75 percent of the players had never voted for a Democrat and that 14 percent think caddies earn too much money. The poll also showed that 23 percent had not attended church in the previous month. Said one unnamed player, "No, I haven't attended church, but the way I'm playing, maybe I'd better."

Better leave the pin in when hitting short shots from off the green. A research team hit thousands of balls with the pin in and out. If you leave the pin in, you'll improve your chance of a hole-out by 34 percent.

On average, Tour players hit only seven fairways per round and 12 greens in regulation. They make only 50 percent of their six-footers.

The odds of beating your handicap by three shots are 200 to 1, according to Dean Knuth, a former statistician at the United States Golf Association. The odds of beating it by five shots jump to 500 to 1. You're looking at more than 1,000,000 to 1 odds of beating it by 10 shots.

Holing Out

According to the Golf Research Group, there were 29,935 golf courses worldwide in 2002. The United States has more golf courses than any other country—more than 17,300. Europe has only 5,850 courses. There are only 100 golf courses in China, for a population of 1.266 billion.

It's estimated that more than 50 million people in the world play golf. Their average score, without any handicap, is 107. Eighty percent of the golfers do not achieve a handicap of less than 18.

For years, Gary Player, a South African, was the only player on the Tour who gave it an international flavor. By 2003 64 international players from 19 countries were members of the PGA Tour.

Tour players earn enough money to buy dual residences, which allows them to time-share charter jet rides to, say, New

Zealand for a weekend and still make it back to America to play an event without missing a beat.

Player, 67, has flown more than 14 million miles in his career and estimates he's spent a total of three and a half to four years sitting in an airline seat. He didn't buy a home in the United States until he began playing the Senior Tour in the 1980s.

There probably is no good place to have a heart attack, but the evidence suggests that a golf course is an especially bad place for one. Golf courses are among the top five public places in America where heart attacks occur.

The logistical difficulty of a paramedic's reaching a fallen golfer in time out on a distant green considerably lowers the victim's odds. According to a recent study by Florida cardiologist Ed Palank, the survival rate of golf course heart attack victims is a "distressingly low" 5 percent.

That's why *Golf Digest* and the American Heart Association have teamed up to get more automated external defibrillators (AEDs) on our nation's golf courses. "After six or eight minutes, the only way someone can be saved is by being defibrillated," says Dr. Palank. The American Heart Association estimates that with a defibrillator, heart attack victims' survival rate can improve to as much as 45 percent.

Back in the roaring '90s, the Dow Jones always roared louder when Tiger roared.

The stock market consistently jumped on Mondays after Woods played televised golf in the United States. The Dow gained about 1.2 percent each time Woods competed, creating

$45 billion in wealth, not all of it going into Tiger's paws, though you might think it did.

Of course, that was the '90s when the two things you could count on were Tiger winning and the Dow going up, up, up. In the early part of the twenty-first century everything's different—except that Tiger keeps winning.